Mad About Movies Number 7

Editors
Gary J. Svehla
Susan Svehla

Graphic Design Interior
Gary J. Svehla

Cover Design
Susan Svehla

Copy Editor
Susan Svehla

Contributing Writers
Anthony Ambrogio;
Nick Anez
Gary J. Svehla

Acknowledgments
Warner Home Video; Fox Home Video;
Universal Home Video; Bender Helper
Publicity; Scott Essman;
Heritage Auction; Movie Goods

Publisher
Midnight Marquee Press, Inc.

Mad About Movies
Number 7
October 2009
Copyright 2009© by Gary J. Svehla

Published irregularly for $10 per issue by Midnight Marquee Press, Inc.

Articles and art should be transmitted electonically and will remain the property of the writer/artist and copyright holder, who will retain the rights. If material intended for publication is sent to us via regular mail, it is the sender's responsibility to include return postage. No responsibility is taken for unsolicited material.

Editorial views expressed by writers are not necessarily those of the publisher, Midnight Marquee Press. Nothing from the magazine may be reproduced or shared in any media without the expressed written permission of the publisher. The Midnight Marquee Press offices are located at: 9721 Britinay Lane, Parkville, MD 21234; website: http://www.midmar.com; e-mail: midmargary@aol.com

Letters of comment addressed to Midnight Marquee or Susan and Gary Svehla will be considered for publication unless the writer requests otherwise.

Letters of comment are encouraged; please send all comments to midmargary@aol.com and label your comments "Comments for *Mad About Movies* issue #7."

We are always looking for new writers to submit articles. Please discuss any article suggestions first with Gary J. Svehla at midmargary@aol.com and check the Style Sheet link on our website to get ideas for style and formatting. Length of articles may vary. We take them long and short. But remember, our emphasis is mainly on the classics of the Golden Age, but our definition of classic and Golden Age is not based upon specific decades or year of production necessarily, but upon the artistic content that reflects the heart and style of early horror cinema.

Copies are mailed, within the USA, for the cost of the issue plus $6 for Media Mail; $10 for Priority Mail. Issues are sent in sturdy mailers, so they should arrive at your home in near mint condition. Foreign orders are welcome, but shipping costs vary. Check with us. We accept all credit cards, PayPal and money orders.

TABLE OF CONTENTS

2   *Mad About Movies* Editorial
      by Gary J. Svehla

3   From *Rio Bravo* to *El Dorado*:
      Journey from Light to Darkness
      by Nick Anez

14   John Ford and
      Two Rode Together
      by Anthony Ambrogio

22   Mad About DVDs Reviews
      by Gary J. Svehla

Mad About Movies Editorial

Welcome to the new look *Mad About Movies*, featuring a full color format that should appear hopefully in mailboxes more frequently. The theme of the current issue is lesser-known Westerns directed by iconic Western directors, in this case John Ford and Howard Hawks. Hawks, famed for his classic Western *Rio Bravo*, is often criticized for going to the well one time too often, in this case with his film *El Dorado*. But writer Nick Anez argues that *El Dorado* is one of Ford's unsung classic movies. Likewise, writer Anthony Ambrogio compares the disparaged *Two Rode Together* to the classic *The Searchers* and demonstrates why *Two Rode Together* is a film waiting to be re-discovered. Ford and Hawks are two giants of American cinema and their lesser-discussed films are not as incidental or minor as first believed.

Rounding out the issue are our in depth DVD reviews. Since it's been a while since the last issue of *Mad About Movies* appeared, some of the DVDs might be a few years old, but hopefully as we return to a more regular publishing schedule, we will catch up with recently released movies. Just give us a little time.

It is becoming increasingly more difficult to maintain a hard print publication such as *Mad About Movies*. We flirted with making our companion magazine *Midnight Marquee* an online *only* magazine, and the current issue #76 was an issue I was proud of, in full color, but published only on the web. People came out of the woodwork to voice their concerns. Think of the trouble it would be to print out the magazine, and then take it to Kinko's to bind…and the expense! People, perhaps justifiably so, stated how difficult it is to read anything substantial on a computer monitor. And while printing out the magazine's pages is not expensive or difficult, making those printed pages permanent and collectible was a challenge. We even offered bound copies for sale, but the time it took Sue to produce these issues was prohibitive. So we decided, after the fact, to produce a hard copy version of issue #76, one that was similar to our original layout but not quite the same (switching from color to black and white was painful to me, after I saw how much depth color added). I missed the creative challenge of working with full color when producing that hard copy edition.

So we debated doing a 90-something page version of *Mad About Movies*, in our smaller 6 by 9 inch size, in glorious black and white (except for covers). Or, we could continue the full color layout with a large-size format, but with fewer pages. We decided that the full color format would be the most attractive to fans, and even if many classic movies are not in color, all classic movies have colorful ads and posters, lobby cards and stills. We would be just about the only current classic film magazine that is printed full color, giving us a commercial edge and an added appeal.

Once again, while many magazines and newspapers that I subscribe to continue to fall by the wayside, or others are switching from a hard print version to an online only version, we will continue to struggle to produce a magazine that fans can hold, feel and, yes, even smell…and also collect. But we need the continued help of classic movie fans to publish in this manner. We thank you for your support in the past, and we thank you for your commitment to the future.

Gary J. Svehla

From Rio Bravo to El Dorado

A Journey from Light to Darkness

by Nick Anez

"Eldorado"   by Edgar Allan Poe

Gaily bedight, A gallant knight
In sunshine and in shadow
Had journeyed long, Singing a song
In search of Eldorado

But he grew old – This knight so bold
And o'er his heart a shadow
Fell as he found No spot of ground
That looked like Eldorado.

And, as his strength Failed him at length
He met a pilgrim shadow –
'Shadow', said he, 'Where can it be –
This land of Eldorado?'

'Over the Mountains of the Moon,
Down the Valley of the Shadow,
Ride, boldly ride' the shade replied –
'If you seek Eldorado!'

John Wayne and Howard Hawks collaborated on five motion pictures. The first was *Red River* in 1948, a Western that was a critical and commercial success. The epic tale of a cattle drive marked by love, obsession and betrayal has retained classic status, despite some criticism over its ending.

Eleven years later, Wayne and Hawks reunited for another western, *Rio Bravo*, which critics patronized as a rather conventional oater. But its reputation steadily increased over the years as critics discerned the film's primary themes of friendship and professionalism beneath the deceptively simple plot, demonstrating the director's expertise at storytelling.

The director and star waited only three years before their next collaboration, the African wildlife adventure, *Hatari*. Also misjudged upon release, this movie has also subsequently achieved acclaim as one of the director's finest works. The film is a superficially simple story of a group of people working together and gradually earning each other's respect and admiration through a series of trials. But yet, as in all movies by Hawks, so much exists beneath the surface. It is also an extremely pleasing mixture of adventure, comedy and romance, all served up in a highly professional manner.

Four years later, Hawks and Wayne reunited once again for their third Western. This one, called *El Dorado*, would be dismissed by many critics who used such words as "predictable" and "standard" to describe it. But this movie would also be accused of plagiarism, not of another director's works, but of the same director's own *Rio Bravo*. Due to similarities of themes and characterizations, Hawks would be accused of copying scenes from the earlier film to hopefully emulate its commercial success. Even today, in movie reference books, *El Dorado* is often listed as a "remake" or "rehashing" of *Rio Bravo*.

However, while there are similarities between the two movies, such similarities are deliberate and serve to make valid points that specifically illustrate the differences of the respective films. Hawks was remarkably innovative in using variations of familiar situations among disparate groups of people to illustrate

the totally dissimilar themes of each movie. The two movies are as different as, literally, night and day.

First, it will be helpful to provide a brief summary of the two movies. *Rio Bravo* begins with a justifiably famous sequence with no dialogue. Joe Burdette (Claude Akins), brother of powerful rancher Nathan Burdette (John Russell), is raising hell in a saloon, looking for trouble. Former lawman Dude (Dean Martin), now the disgraced town drunk, is desperate enough for a drink to be humiliated by Joe, but Sheriff John T. Chance (John Wayne) will not allow Dude to debase himself. Chance's reward is to be clubbed unconscious by Dude, who then tries to vent his rage upon Joe. This leads to Joe's brutal murder of a bystander and his arrest by Chance, with a little help from Dude.

The main plot of *Rio Bravo* then kicks in. It is relatively simple, quite similar to the plots of countless other Westerns. Sheriff Chance has to keep Joe in his jail until the U.S. Marshal arrives. But that is not an easy task, since Nathan has an army of gunmen in his employ and proceeds to isolate the sheriff. Chance knows that he needs help if he is going to survive, but he also knows that he needs professionals who are good with a gun.

Unlike a certain lawman by the name of Will Kane in faraway Hadleyville, Chance doesn't ask local townspeople for help because he knows that they would be worthless in a real fight. He refuses the help of well-meaning friends, such as his jailer, Stumpy (Walter Brennan), whom he feels is too crippled and old to take part in a possible gunfight. He also declines the help of wagonmaster Pat Wheeler (Ward Bond), though he senses that Wheeler's young cowhand, Colorado (Ricky Nelson), could be helpful. He knows that Dude was once a dependable deputy, until a wandering petticoat ruined him and turned him into "Barachon," which is Spanish for drunk. However, when Dude came to Chance's aid in his arrest of Joe, it was a sign of a possible turning point for the former deputy. Chance, as much out of friendship as duty, decides to once again put his trust in Dude, while keeping a weary eye on him.

In the meantime, Chance has to deal with a professional gambler in town, a woman named Feathers (Angie Dickinson), who has the reputation of being a cardsharp. When Chance turns out to be wrong about Feathers, he refuses to admit his mistake, since he disapproves of her line of work. Almost against his will, Chance finds himself both annoyed by, and attracted to, Feathers, but he still rejects her offer to help. He doesn't have any more use for a woman in a fight than he does for Stumpy or for Carlos, owner of the hotel in which Chance lives. He doesn't want amateurs getting in his way.

After a few skirmishes, Chance soon realizes that the best strategy is to remain in the jail until the marshal arrives. Chance, Dude, Colorado and Stumpy then maintain the jail as a fort, while Burdette and his men lay siege to the lawmen. Dude even agrees to take a bath, finally shedding the filthy clothing of a town drunkard. But he remains edgy and unsure of himself, despite Chance's guidance. When Dude is overpowered and captured by the opposition, Burdette proposes an exchange of prisoners. Chance has no recourse but to agree to the exchange to save Dude's life.

With Chance and his group facing Burdette and his men, the two prisoners start walking toward one another. But Dude tackles Joe, leading to a fierce gun battle between the two forces. Thanks to the help of Stumpy as well as Carlos and even the recently gunned down Wheeler, all of whom Chance didn't think he needed, Chance and his men win the day and justice is served.

Returning hired gun Cole Thornton (John Wayne) receives a warm welcome from former flame, Maudie (Charlene Holt).

J.P. Harrah (Robert Mitchum) is not very pleased with Cole Thornton's method of sobering him up.

With peace restored to Rio Bravo, Chance begrudgingly admits his love for Feathers, while Dude and Stumpy maintain law and order in the town.

The simple plot is deceiving but secondary to the main themes of the movie, which concern the characters and their relationships. Beneath the familiar plot lies subjects which are important to Hawks, primarily the manner in which a group of individuals join together to help one another and achieve a specific goal. During the course of the adventure, they will develop mutual respect as well as acceptance of one another's faults. And the journey is usually accompanied by the main character's romantic attraction to a woman, who brings her own skills to the mix.

Rio Bravo brings these themes together in a superb manner by a director who has as much expertise as the characters in his movies. As the group becomes interdependent, each person learns that relationships and tolerance of others' deficiencies are as important as independence and self-respect. Most significantly, the film's hero, Chance, learns that he is perhaps too inflexible and has set standards for others that may be too high. While he was correct in his assessments of Dude and Colorado, he had misjudged both Stumpy and Feathers. And the dynamite that helped to win the battle belonged to his friend Wheeler. Chance, much to his own surprise, discovers that he needed others just as much as they needed him.

Rio Bravo was a major commercial success, but most critics greeted the film with classic indifference, missing the subtlety of the Hawksian themes and condescendingly assuming that the movie was just another John Wayne Western, and not a very original one at that. (Many had the same attitude three years earlier upon the release of John Ford's *The Searchers*.) They accused Wayne of playing Wayne, missing the subtle nuances and the underlying emotion beneath his command of his character. Wayne is the center of the film, and though the overtly dramatic scenes belong to the other actors, his understated authority exerts control over the characters and the entire film.

Martin's superb performance, his breakthrough role as a dramatic actor, was also ignored. (In his previous dramatic film, *The Young Lions*, he had essentially played himself.) The scene in which he seems to be on the verge of having a drink, and then pours the whiskey back into the bottle, is a highpoint. Equally fine and neglected is Walter Brennan's memorable portrayal of Stumpy. The conflicting emotions of anger, fear and anxiety he displays when he accidentally fires at Dude is a masterful example of acting.

However, since many critics were notoriously biased against Westerns, they ignored the film's impeccable qualities. Furthermore, those critics pompously opined, how could anyone seriously review a Western in which two popular singers played

Sheriff J.P. Harrah washes away the sins of his past, as friends Cole Thornton and Maudie look on, in this publicity shot.

key roles? And Hawks even had the temerity to include a scene in which they shared a song! Shades of Gene Autry and Roy Rogers.

It was only with the passage of time that the reputation of the movie gradually increased to the point where it is now considered a classic. It is a totally entertaining movie with action and thrills, as well as tenderness and emotion. It is the kind of movie that can be watched over and over again. It's like returning to old friends whose company is always gratifying. Chance, Dude, Stumpy, Feathers are all so real and pleasant that it is always a delight to spend time with them. There aren't any more characters like them, certainly not in movies.

Colorado doesn't quite measure up to the others in part because Ricky Nelson's acting tended to be somewhat wooden, though the sheer professionalism of his co-stars carries him along. Nelson's inexperience doesn't harm the movie for another reason. Of the four men and woman that form the close-knit group, Colorado is the only one that doesn't have a screen history that impacts upon the progress of the movie.

Chance implies to Feathers that he was once a gunfighter and that being a lawman has brought meaning to his life, which provides a thematic reason for his rigidity. Dude's past experience with a woman has turned him into a pitiable figure, but it is that same experience that leads to his need for redemption. Feathers' reputation will have a definite impact upon the humanizing of Chance. And Stumpy may initially appear to be comic relief, but his key scene occurs when Burdette tries to resolve the impasse with Chance. In a brief exchange with Burdette, Stumpy reveals that he used to be a landowner until Burdette apparently forced him off his property. Stumpy's bitter words are enlightening in particular because he calls Burdette by his first name, indicating that they may have at one time been friends. *Rio Bravo* has numerous equally meaningful scenes, all of which add up to pristine entertainment.

Three years after *Rio Bravo*, Hawks and Wayne had another huge commercial success with *Hatari*. Wayne followed that African movie with other box-office hits (including Henry Hathaway's *The Sons of Katie Elder*, in which he re-teamed with Dean Martin.) However, Hawks' next two movies, *Man's Favorite Sport* with Rock Hudson and *Red Line 7000* with a cast of young unknowns, both bombed, the latter film perhaps being the nadir of the director's career. So he and the Duke reunited for a fourth time and, according to myth, recycled elements from *Rio Bravo* for their third Western.

In 1967, *El Dorado* was released. This movie begins with another significant scene that sets up the movie. Sheriff J.P. Harrah (Robert Mitchum) walks down the main street of El Dorado, rifle in hand. He enters a saloon and is directed by the bartender to the washroom. Inside, he finds Cole Thornton (John Wayne), a gunfighter who is surprised to see Harrah's rifle aimed at his chest. Harrah explains that land baron Bart Jason (Ed Asner), who has hired Cole, is forcing smaller ranchers off their property and that Cole and Harrah are on opposite sides. Realizing that he has been deceived by Jason, Cole tells Harrah that he will decline the job. Harrah is relieved and the two men greet one another with fondness. Since they will not be trying to kill one another, they can resume their friendship, despite the sudden appearance of Maudie (Charlene Holt), a woman who appears to be close to both Harrah and Cole.

Cole visits Jason at his ranch and refuses his offer of a job. Fatefully, Jason's adversary, rancher Kevin MacDonald, has been alerted of Cole's appearance in town and puts his family on guard. MacDonald makes the fatal mistake of sending his youngest son, Luke, to stand lookout for Cole, and Cole shoots the boy unintentionally. After Cole tries to tend to Luke, the boy kills himself to end his pain. Cole, grief-stricken, brings the boy's body back to his family. In retaliation, MacDonald's daughter, Joey, follows Cole and ambushes him. Cole, a bullet wound in his back, cannot kill another MacDonald child, particularly a girl, and furiously sends her back to her father. After recuperating and being told by the town's elderly doctor that the bullet in his back will have to be removed by a specialist, Cole bids farewell to Harrah and Maudie and leaves El Dorado to look for another job.

Several months pass and Cole is passing through a town in which he witnesses a confrontation between a young man called Mississippi (James Caan) and a group of men led by professional gunman Nelse McLeod (Christopher George). Cole saves the life of Mississippi, who is good with a knife but inexperienced with a gun. Cole and McLeod, both skilled professionals, express cautious respect for one another and go their separate ways, but not until after McLeod mentions that he is on his way to work for Bart Jason. More significantly, McLeod tells Cole that Harrah has become a drunk. With Mississippi trailing along, Cole heads back to El Dorado to try to help his old friend.

Up to this point, no similarity to *Rio Bravo* exists. Characterizations and plot are dissimilar. Yes, the Hawksian themes of friendship, professionalism and a hint of a romance with a strong woman are present, but the characterizations are not imitative in any sense. Wayne's character is not a lawman but a gunfighter. Unlike John T. Chance, Cole has remained a hired gunfighter, not having found the meaning in his life that Chance found.

The similarities begin once Cole arrives back in El Dorado. Cole finds that Sheriff Harrah, who in some respects was initially a descendant of Chance, has indeed now become a drunk, a descendant of Dude. Like Dude, the cause of his downfall was a woman and he has become an equally pathetic object of scorn and ridicule in the town he once served so nobly.

Other similarities to the earlier film subsequently creep into the plot. The range war between the MacDonalds and Bart Jason's gang, though not similar to the earlier film's plot of a

lawman versus a rancher, has heated up and serves as the nominal plot. However, once again, this is a pretext for the director's concerns of relationships, professionalism and group solidarity. Cole, out of friendship for Harrah, assumes the job of defender of the ranchers against Jason and McLeod, while doing his best to restore his friend's integrity in the community. And when Bart Jason is arrested and held in jail, once again a siege takes place, followed by an exchange of prisoners and a final battle.

It sure does sound familiar. Substitute Cole Thornton for John T. Chance, J.P. Harrah for Dude and Mississippi for Colorado. For goodness sake, did the young men both have to be named after a state? It was as though Hawks was deliberately trying to draw attention to the similarities. There is even a running joke about Harrah having to take a bath, much like Dude. And instead of Stumpy, we have Bull Thomas, an equally cantankerous but

John Wayne's conflicted and tainted anti-hero Cole Thornton makes *El Dorado* a Western that resonates.

resourceful old geezer. Arthur Hunnicut plays Bull, who was Hawks' second choice after Walter Brennan became unavailable.

This, as many critics wrote, was obviously a case of a formerly talented director stealing from one of his biggest hits to try to reclaim some of his old glory. Since the earlier movie was a commercial success, such critics argue, here is a formerly talented director playing the box-office game and displaying for all to see just how unoriginal he had become.

Hawks definitely borrowed scenes and elements from *Rio Bravo* for *El Dorado*. Besides the alcoholic character and the siege of the jail, there is also the manner in which the drunk begins his redemption by shooting a killer in a saloon, very reminiscent of a scene in the earlier film. Hawks didn't try to conceal these similarities while creating the latter film. What is significant is that he re-uses *familiar* situations to illustrate *differences* in characterization.

Incidentally, Leigh Brackett shares screenplay credit with Jules Furthman on the earlier film and receives sole credit for the later film. However, in both cases, Hawks supervised the writing, being the auteur of his most personal films. (Both screenplays are essentially original ones, despite the credit to a story by B.H. McCampbell for *Rio Bravo* and a novel by Harry Brown for *El Dorado*; McCampbell was Hawks' daughter and Brown was livid that the film bore no relation to his novel.) And it should be remembered that plot is secondary to Hawks and that characterizations propel his films. In this respect, the films are totally dissimilar, not only pertaining to the characters but, more significantly, to their state of body and mind.

Rio Bravo is a glorious adventure of one good man in his physical prime enlisting the aid of other good men to fight evil, while restoring his best friend to stability. The film's suspense derives from the conflict between the heroes and the villains. After certain travails, the good men emerge triumphant due to the inherent nobility of their hearts and souls. The hero reaffirms his own strength, while learning to appreciate the strengths of others. His colleagues rediscover their own strengths as well as their self-respect. The movie is filled with warmth that is infectious to audiences and leaves a good feeling.

In contrast, *El Dorado* is a tragedy of one aging man past his prime trying to battle evil, while restoring his friend, also past his prime, to stability. The movie has suspense and tension, due particularly to the failing capabilities of its two main characters, as well as to the conflict between the aging hero and the younger gunfighter, whose proficiency may surpass the older man's. Eventually, the two flawed heroes find that their capabilities and resources are just not up to the job and, though they emerge triumphant, it is at a great price to their hearts and their souls. The movie is essentially a tragedy that leaves a feeling of sadness.

Rio Bravo's John T. Chance is the epitome of a Western lawman. He is brave and seemingly invulnerable. He has skills which he uses to serve others in the town he has chosen to call his home. He enjoys his profession and is satisfied with his life, despite its risks. He is the rock upon whom all the others gather around and draw their strength from. He is also a true friend to Dude, who has fallen to pieces because of his weakness of character. If Chance has a flaw, it is that he is quick to judge those who do not meet his standards. He misjudges Feathers and is bluntly cruel to Stumpy, to keep him from getting hurt. But these human failings will set him up for his humanization and do not detract from his inherent dignity.

El Dorado's Cole Thornton lives by his gun, not by the law. He sells his skills for money. He has no home and journeys from one place to another, wherever his next job may take him. Like Chance, he values friendship and when he learns that J.P. Harrah has fallen hard, he wastes no time going to his aid. But it is a tortuous journey. Unlike Chance, Cole is saddled with vulnerabilities and eventually will be dependent upon others. He suffers from the wound inflicted upon him by Joey MacDonald, a wound which causes sudden spurts of pain that render him increasingly helpless with each attack. His crippling is also psychological, for the guilt of killing Luke MacDonald weighs heavily upon him. He is dissatisfied with his life and looks upon El Dorado as a means to bring meaning into his life, through not only helping Harrah but also the MacDonalds, to make up for taking the life of Luke. And there's Maudie, waiting patiently and longingly for him.

In the town of Rio Bravo, as the conflict builds gradually to the climactic gun battle, John T. Chance never wavers or displays any sign of weakness. Most of the skirmishes take place during the day because Chance is the kind of person who has a code of honor and plays by the rules. The Burdettes don't believe in codes, as evident from Joe's murder of an innocent man and the

Burdette gang's murder of Wheeler. Chance's strength inspires every person in his group. Dude knows that Chance has placed his faith in him and it is this faith that gives him the strength to redeem himself. The final battle between good and evil takes place in the blazing sun, where every man's movements can be seen and judged.

In the town of El Dorado, once again the conflict builds gradually from one skirmish to another. But due to Cole's vulnerability, Jason's gang captures him. It is significant that, in this film, it is not the former drunk whose weakness leads to his capture, but the actions of leader himself, Cole Thornton, whose infirmity has placed the group and their quest for justice in jeopardy. He is, in effect, as crippled as Harrah. Cole and Harrah know that they are not the men they once were and are trying to recapture some of their former dignity. Their bodies have deteriorated and this may be their last chance for salvation, their last chance to prove not only to the people depending upon them but to themselves that they are worthy of respect.

Cole gives old friend J.P. Harrah an opportunity to regain his self-respect, while Bull Harris (Arthur Hunnicutt) looks on.

Also of significance is the fact that the young member of the group, Mississippi, lacks the skills of Colorado. He cannot use a gun and must be given a shotgun to give him an edge over an opponent, a form of cheating. This is another deliberate irony in view of his proud statement at the beginning of the movie that his mentor didn't have to cheat at gambling because he was too good. Mississippi's deficiencies, in contrast to Colorado's professionalism, are another indication of the inferiority of the small-knit group, compared to *Rio Bravo*'s group, that eventually will be formed.

Mississippi, unlike Colorado, doesn't have to be persuaded to join the group but joins voluntarily to journey with Cole to El Dorado. The journey on horseback leads to the scene during which Mississippi recites Edgar Allan Poe's poem "Eldorado."

Mississippi (James Chan) and Joey MacDonald (Michelle Carey) frolic in the hay, in a very hot publicity shot.

Cole doesn't understand the significance of the words but it will soon become clear that Cole will forever be riding "Over the mountains of the Moon" in his endless quest to reach, not the town of El Dorado, but the fabled land itself. (Hawks dismissed any artistic significance to the poem's inclusion in the film but he, like Ford, frequently denied literary allusions, as though perhaps embarrassed by them. Despite the director's dismissal, the allusions to the poem's theme in the movie, as well as in the film's title song, are simply too numerous to ignore.)

Cole's infirmity and Mississippi's inadequacies are only the first indications that the final gun battle will not be the fair fight that took place in *Rio Bravo*. In a fair fight, Cole and his group would probably lose and this is made clear throughout the movie, particularly when both Cole and Harrah are contrasted with Nelse McLeod. Nelse is the man that Cole perhaps used to be. Physically, Nelse is at the height of his powers. He also has scruples and insists on playing by the rules. He doesn't like the fact that it took three men to kill Mississippi's mentor. Like Cole, he is disgusted by the lack of fairness displayed by even his own men and he intends to see that Bart Jason plays by his rules. He believes in "professional courtesy" and looks forward to facing Cole in a fair fight, if only to find out who is the better man.

However, it is Cole Thornton who doesn't play by the rules. The final gun battle, like so many other scenes in the movie, takes place at night, as though Cole doesn't want any witnesses to what he knows he must do to survive. Unable to use his crippled arm and suffering from pain, Cole doesn't give Nelse any chance at all in their final duel. He doesn't extend the professional courtesy that McLeod has just extended to him and cheats in a way that borders on cold-blooded murder.

The subsequent battle between Thornton's group and the Jason gang is brutal and few of Jason's gang are left alive. Once again, it is significant that Jason is killed not by Cole or Harrah, but by Joey, who atones for her shooting of Cole by saving his

should have researched Western lore. In the Old West, it was not unusual for cowboys to sit around singing and strumming guitars to entertain themselves or even to relieve stress. But this may be irrelevant as far as Hawks is concerned. The bottom line is that it adds to the pleasure of the movie.)

In *Rio Bravo*, warmth pervades the entire movie because of the characterizations and their developing relationships. The pleasant camaraderie that slowly develops seems to be a natural extension of admirable and decent people uniting for a common cause. Chance never wavers in his confidence, despite overwhelming odds, and his faith in the men he has chosen to help him is ultimately justified, while his lack of faith in specific others humbles him. The climactic confrontation takes place during the day with the bright sun illuminating their heroism and nobility. The movie is, in essence, a journey from the darkness of the violent introduction to the light of victory, friendship and love.

In contrast, a sense of sadness permeates throughout *El Dorado*. It is Cole's instinctive killing of Luke MacDonald that sets the tone of this film, despite the humorous scenes that occur in the middle part of the film, primarily regarding the curing of Harrah's alcoholism. Luke MacDonald is never forgotten, not only because of the guilt that burdens Cole, but because it was this killing that resulted in Cole's crippling. The killing of Luke is poignant, but the following scene at the Macdonald ranch is even more powerful. It is an extremely heartrending yet understated scene because of the stoic manner in which not only Cole but most of the MacDonald family react to the death of the boy. The memory of the scene haunts the entire movie, just as it haunts Cole.

Because of his failing capabilities, Cole lacks the self-confidence of Chance and soon realizes, that if he is going to survive, he will have to break the rules that he has always lived by. He is going to have to lower himself to the level of Bart Jason (or Joe Burdette), life. Even after killing McLeod unfairly, Cole is still rendered helpless as Jason prepares to gun him down.

There is a sense of joy throughout *Rio Bravo*, despite the violent introduction and the deadly skirmishes. The humorous byplays between Chance and Feathers are typical of Hawks, since the woman often has the upper hand in his films and it is amusing to see the invincible Chance embarrassed. It is also pleasant to see him gradually fall under the spell of Feathers, even though he knows that he will have to complete his job before even entertaining a notion of romance. Even more amusing are the antics of Stumpy, whose irascibility, everyone knows, masks a good heart.

However, it is the celebrated, and often disparaged, song sequence that is the key to the movie. This is the scene that officially certifies the group as a family. It is deliberate that Chance, who maintains his status as group leader, doesn't join in but looks on approvingly as Dude, Colorado and Stumpy sing along. (Incidentally, critics harped on this scene as a sign of Hawks' shameless attempt to cater to the commercial demands of audiences, specifically fans of Nelson and Martin. They something John T. Chance would never do and something that Nelse McLeod would never do. This movie is a journey from the green meadows of the opening scenes to the darkness that envelops the final battle and that exists within Cole's soul.

It is also interesting that Nelse McLeod is not an unlikable character, despite being on the wrong side of the law. Nelse projects the integrity and honor that isn't possessed anymore by Cole. His death is regrettable and it is a tribute to Hawks and the actors that such a radical element was injected into the movie. It is radical not only because the villain is more admirable than the heroes, but because he is killed unfairly by John Wayne, the icon. Equally unsettling to the Duke's image is the scene in which, after being crippled by an attack, he is tied and gagged by the enemy in a way that makes him more helpless and defenseless than in his entire film canon. In addition, this scene is preceded by one in which he cowers to safety under a hanging rock after once again being crippled by an attack.

It is an accepted fact that Wayne would do just about anything for both John Ford and Howard Hawks, feeling eternally grateful

On the road to El Dorado Cole tries to teach Mississippi gun skills while the younger man recites Poe's poem about the search for the legendary land of the same name.

to them for two of his breakthrough films (*Stagecoach* and *Red River*). But it was his respect for the directors and trust in them that persuaded the Duke to alter his image so drastically. His portrayal of the hatred-obsessed Ethan Edwards in *The Searchers* has been extensively discussed and analyzed, as much for the sheer force of Wayne's acting as for the departure from his usual screen image.

In a way, his portrayal of Cole Thornton is just as radical, though it has not received the extensive analysis of his earlier portrayal. Cole's killing of Luke MacDonald was unintentional, since he fired instinctively at someone whom he believed fired at him. But the fact is that Luke was confused and scared, firing not at Cole but as a warning. In partial defense of Cole, he didn't know that.

Cole's killing of Nelse McLeod is less excusable. When Cole grabs his rifle and repeatedly fires at the totally surprised gunman, he violates not only his own personal code of honor but John Wayne's as well. As the dying McLeod chastises Cole for not giving him a chance, Cole's only response is that he couldn't fight fairly because Nelse was too good; sadly, Cole had to cheat to win. McLeod's dying expression reflects disappointment in his adversary; Cole's expression reflects shame. In effect this act will doom Cole even more than his killing of Luke MacDonald, and his expression indicates awareness of this.

The last scene of *Rio Bravo* is a humorous one, depicting Dude and Stumpy walking down the town's main street. They are enjoying the reward of renewed self-esteem, while Chance enjoys a romantic moment with Feathers. They are all better persons because of the experiences they have shared. The last scene of *El Dorado* also depicts two men walking down the town's main street. This scene also is played for humor as both Cole and Harrah hobble down the street on crutches. However, implicit is the sense that both Cole and Harrah will never be whole again. They have emerged triumphant but at the expense of their honor and sense of justice. They will forever be crippled, if not physically then psychologically.

Once again, Wayne's superb portrayal was ignored. The agony he projects during his attacks is so real that it is almost painful to watch. In the scene in which he comes upon Luke MacDonald, writhing in pain, his reaction reflects shock, sorrow and shame as he quickly holsters his gun. And the fury he displays after being shot by Joey, as he rubs his blood onto her shirt, is frightening in its potential for violence. Wayne's performance is a masterful one.

Equally fine is Mitchum. As in the earlier film, the drunk has most of the overtly dramatic scenes and Mitchum is outstanding. He projects pathos and self-pity as an alcoholic, pride and nobility as a lawman. The scene at the saloon in which he projects all of these conflicting emotions as he tries to summon up his past dignity, puffing up his chest behind the torn and dirty clothing, is only one example of a truly superb performance. But Mitchum, like Wayne, (and, for that matter, Hawks), was always taken for granted. A flawless cast supports Mitchum and Wayne, but Christopher George deserves special praise for his compelling portrayal of Nelse McLeod.

Music is an essential part of both movies and also helps to set the tone for the films and their characters. The main title theme of *Rio Bravo*, composed by Dimitri Tiomkin, is a pleasant melody that suggests the enjoyable, leisurely film that is about to take place. Paul Francis Webster's lyrics to the tune suggest a lost romance and the longing of a cowboy for true love. These are pleasant lyrics that originally were intended to be heard over the credits. But they would have set the wrong tone for the movie since Dude cannot long for the woman that caused his downfall, and Chance would deny any hint of such longing. So Hawks eliminated the lyrics from the movie, except for a couple of lines that accompany the end credits. Retained for the movie, though, is the song shared by Martin and Nelson called "My Rifle, My Pony and Me." This is an equally pleasant ballad that expresses the wish of a cowboy for friendships to alleviate his loneliness. It is perfectly appropriate to the theme of camaraderie that propels the film.

The music for *El Dorado* is composed by Nelson Riddle and, in this film, the lyrics to the title tune are heard because they are a perfect representation of the film's theme. If there is any doubt as to the director's intentions for this movie, as contrasted with his intentions for the earlier movie, the theme song makes them quite clear. Using Poe's poem as an inspiration, John Gabriel's lyrics express the longing of a man who is always searching for the fabled land of El Dorado. He knows there is something more to life than what he can see and is constantly trying to find the end of the rainbow, never losing sight of his dream despite growing older and more tired. The rich baritone voice of George Alexander, backed by The Mellowmen, resonates with yearning and maturity. The song is as bittersweet and sad as the movie that will follow.

There is one other illustration of the differences of the two movies and that is the imagined fate of the main characters that inhabited the towns of Rio Bravo and El Dorado, after the film's story has concluded.

In *Rio Bravo*, John T. Chance expressed his love for Feathers at the end of the movie by threatening to arrest her, if she wore her revealing costume in public. As he takes her in his arms, he has probably already made the decision to settle down, give up his job as sheriff and perhaps live on a small ranch near town.

As for Dude, he will succeed Chance as town sheriff and will serve with such distinction, for so long, that everyone will totally forget that he was once called "Barachon." He may even settle down with a good woman, having acquired wisdom and strength of character. It is not inconceivable to imagine Dude and his bride frequently visiting the Chances on their ranch to reminisce about old times, when the West was wild and the town of Rio Bravo was untamed. Maybe Stumpy will even get his land back.

In *El Dorado*, the tone of the movie is simply too bleak to suggest a happy ending for anyone, other than minor characters. The MacDonalds can live a peaceful life and Mississippi will settle down with Joey. They were all fighting for justice, not for self-esteem, which is far more difficult to attain, once it is lost. And the idealism of lost youth is impossible to recapture. Bull knows this better than anyone and can only shake his head in sorrow over the eventual fate of his two friends.

J.P. Harrah, unlike Dude, never quite learned from his past mistakes. He was older than Dude, too old to change. It would not be at all surprising if he fell for another wandering petticoat and fell off the wagon once again. He as much admits this to old Bull. The crutch he leans on at the end of *El Dorado* is symptomatic of his emotional infirmity. Though Maudie may have pity on him, others may well start calling him "Barachon."

Mississippi avenges the death of his mentor by displaying his skill with a knife.

As for Cole Thornton, the restlessness and the longing will return. Though he has found temporary peace in the town of El Dorado, the El Dorado of his fantasy is beyond his mortal reach. Unlike Chance, it is too late for Cole to respond to the love of a woman. And so Maudie will watch him ride away once again, this time never to return. The end of the rainbow is unattainable, and will always be, particularly for someone burdened with guilt. He has to keep searching for his dream, because it is the search for something that he has lost that keeps him going. He will keep wandering as his body grows older and wearier. Eventually, he will find a lonely place to rest and just not have the strength to rise again. And when he closes his eyes for the last time in the Valley of the Shadow, he will find the El Dorado of his dreams.

Rio Bravo and *El Dorado* are both superb examples of Hollywood filmmaking by one of its finest directors. Only eight years separate the movies, but they represent totally different perspectives on the Old West and the type of legendary persons who tamed it. *Rio Bravo* is an immensely uplifting and enjoyable depiction of heroism, romance and nobility, all immaculately presented as wondrous entertainment. It may or may not have mattered to Hawks that the Old West of *Rio Bravo* is partly mythological, because his West served only as a backdrop for his admirable and likeable characters. *El Dorado* is a darker and more austere vision of the Old West, reflecting not necessarily Hawks' disillusionment with the myth of fantasy, but his understanding that nobility and heroism often were simply not enough to attain victory over evil. More sadly, perhaps, he understood that dignity and idealism too often are corrupted by age and loss.

In 1970, Hawks and Wayne reunited once again for *Rio Lobo*, but the magic didn't work this time. The supporting cast was weak and the script was uneven. Hawks and the Duke had to carry this film alone. Within such a context, the few elements that were "borrowed" from the two earlier movies stood out too plainly. This would prove to be Hawks' last film and, though it has its followers and is worth seeing, is ultimately disappointing. Perhaps indicative of the film's quality is the following often-told anecdote. The Duke had accepted the role without seeing the screenplay, because it was Hawks who wanted him. Upon arriving on the set and reading the script, he smiled at Hawks and asked, "Do I play the drunk this time?"

Howard Hawks made many great films in his career and it is gratifying that *Rio Bravo* is at last recognized as a classic. *El Dorado* hasn't yet reached that plateau, in part because of the superficial similarities to the earlier film, but its reputation has been steadily increasing with the passage of time. In fact, *El Dorado* is as much a classic as *Rio Bravo* and, without taking away any luster from that wonderful earlier film, it may well be Hawks' masterpiece.

John Ford and TWO RODE TOGETHER
by Anthony Ambrogio

Quick! Name a John Ford Western scripted by Frank S. Nugent in which two men seek white prisoners taken by Comanche.

If you answered *The Searchers* (1956), you're half right. *Two Rode Together* (1961), made a scant five years later, employs the same "high concept"—but to a much different effect. And that's part of what makes *Two Rode Together* so fascinating.

We derive pleasure from seeing a talented artist revisit material he or she has explored before. Though we yearn for "originality" in art, we just as often enjoy tracing patterns from work to work: We long for both expectation and surprise. Part of this "pleasure in repetition" may be lost on audiences of the time, who, for example, probably thought Howard Hawks had run out of ideas when he "remade" *Rio Bravo* (1959) as *El Dorado* (1967) and then as *Rio Lobo* (1970). In retrospect, however, Hawks' variations on a theme let us study how his ideas on the same subject changed. But that's another paper, one tackled by Nick Anez, also in this issue.

Time is a crucial factor in evaluating art. While 1950s critics thought that John Ford was losing his touch with his audiences—that his best work was behind him—later critics rank his post-war work as perhaps his best. One of those later critics, Andrew Sarris, speculates that "repetition" might have contributed to these opposite perceptions:

> Through the late Forties and early Fifties, Ford strengthened the impression that he was standing still by turning out no fewer than four remakes of earlier movies. *Three Godfathers* (1948) was a remake of his own *Marked Men* (1919), itself remade in the intervening years by William Wyler (*Hell's Heroes*, 1930) and Richard Boleslavski [sic:Boleslawski] (*Three Godfathers* [aka *Miracle in the Sand*], 1936). *What Price Glory?* was an elegant reprise of Raoul Walsh's earthier 1926 movie from the play by Maxwell Anderson and Laurence Stallings. *The Sun Shines Bright* (1953) was an elaboration of the folk materials of Ford's own *Judge Priest* (1934), and *Mogambo* a relatively "straight" remake of Victor Fleming's zesty 1932 entertainment, *Red Dust*. None of these remakes, however, could be considered routine or mechanical. In each instance, Ford altered the tone, and enlarged the scope of the original. Indeed, the remakes cannot be properly or adequately appreciated unless one is thoroughly familiar with the earlier treatment of the same basic anecdotal material. It is not a question of better or worse, or more or less original, but rather of a shift in stylistic and thematic emphasis. (*The John Ford Movie Mystery* [Bloomington, Indiana: Indiana University Press, 1975], p. 144)

While *Two Rode Together* is not a remake of *The Searchers*, it is a re-thinking of "the same basic anecdotal material," reflecting "a shift in stylistic and thematic emphasis." One can appreciate *Two Rode Together* for itself, but it gains resonance in comparison to *The Searchers*.

The Searchers is Homeric in scope, following the five-year odyssey of Ethan Edwards (John Wayne) and Martin Pauley

(Jeffrey Hunter). *Two Rode Together* does not quite observe the classical Unity of Time (some two weeks pass, though it seems like a few days), but it's still more of a "chamber Western."

The Searchers is epic *and* focused, building dramatically to its culmination: the reclamation of "little Debbie" (Natalie Wood)—and Ethan Edwards' reclamation of his soul. *Two Rode Together* is compressed yet discursive; it redeems its captives well before the film's climax and then examines what happens *after* they're returned to "civilization" (though it, too, is ultimately about the redemption of its protagonist).

The motives in *Two Rode Together* are less "pure" than in *The Searchers*, wherein Ethan is driven to find Debbie by pure vengeance, and Martin is driven by pure love. *Nobody*'s pure in *Two Rode Together*; everyone has ulterior motives.

With the latest Indian wars over and a shaky peace in place, the army enlists the reluctant assistance of cheerfully corrupt Marshal Guthrie McCabe (James Stewart)—who gets 10 percent of everything in town—to negotiate the return of white hostages, whom the Comanche captured years before. McCabe regards this endeavor as a fool's errand, an empty political gesture (the army's pressuring him because Washington is pressuring the army because the electorate is pressuring Washington), but he takes the job for his own un-altruistic reasons. He needs to put some distance between himself and the increasingly marriage-minded woman who keeps him, saloon owner Belle Aragon (Annelle Hayes), and he smells some money to be made on the deal from the settlers desperate for their loved ones' return—or just desperate: The protracted search is costing no-nonsense businessman Henry J. Wringle (Willis Bouchey) both money and time, and time *is* money to Henry J., whose wife married him on condition that he find her now grown son by her first marriage. Wringle offers McCabe $1,000 for the return of *any* boy the right age, so he can quit himself of his promise.

Accompanying McCabe is Lt. Jim Gary (Richard Widmark), who has fallen in love with Marty Purcell (Shirley Jones). She lost a brother to the Indians and blames herself for his abduction, keeping the kidnapped boy's music box as a symbol of her obsessive guilt. McCabe and Gary ride to Indian territory and find several captives who don't want to come back, either because of the humiliation they feel or because they now feel part of the tribe. Chief Quanah Parker (Henry Brandon) covets the repeating rifles McCabe offers in trade, so he trusses up young Running Wolf (David Kent), forcing the boy to go back with the men so McCabe can pass off the youth as Wringle's stepson. He even throws in Elena (Linda Cristal), the Mexican wife of Stone Calf (Woody Strode)—Parker's hated rival—mostly to spite Stone Calf and probably to get rid of him. Stone Calf comes after his squaw, and McCabe kills him—an action for which both Quanah Parker and the army are grateful. Major Frazer (John McIntire), who's expressed only contempt for McCabe and his mercenary ways, tells him that he's performed a service the military couldn't (without breaking the treaty).

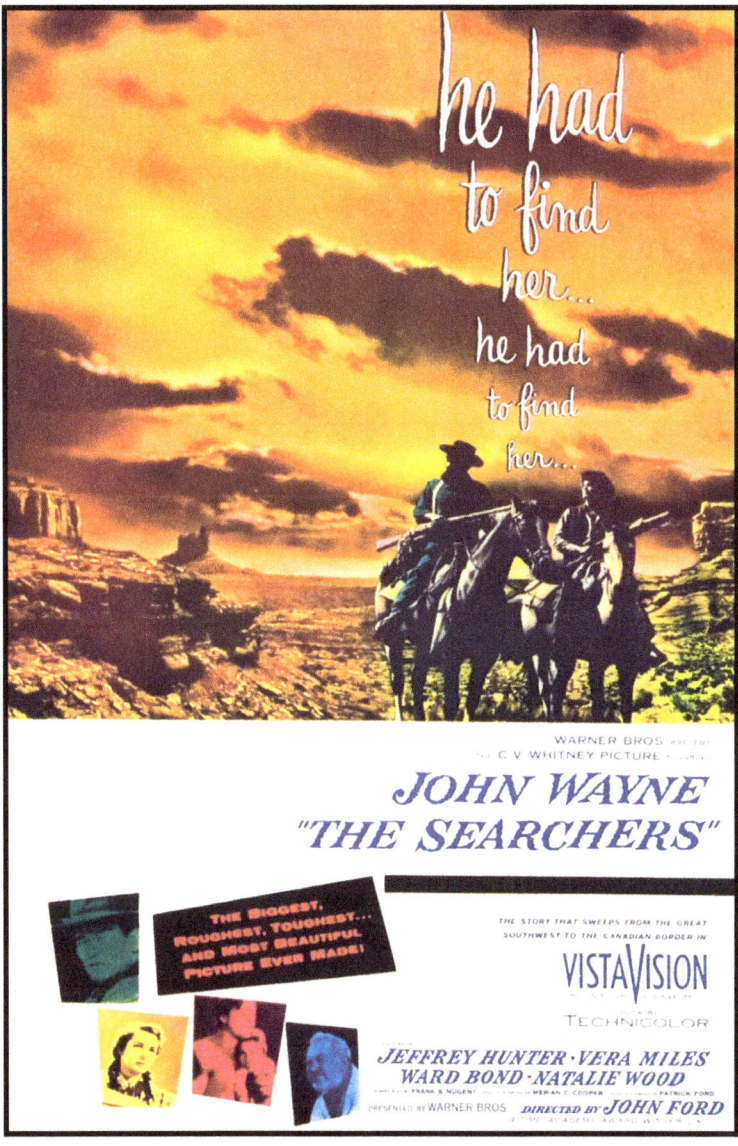

The returned captives have trouble readjusting to white society. (White society has trouble adjusting to *them*.) Elena is an object of outright curiosity and barely disguised contempt for having cohabited with an Indian. McCabe loudly defends her. Running Wolf loudly proclaims himself Comanche. He throws a bucket of water at Wringle, who decides the boy's *not* his stepson after all, and reneges on his deal with McCabe. Mrs. McCandless (Jeanette Nolan), unhinged since her own child's kidnapping, insists Running Wolf is her lost son; she and her doting husband (Cliff Lyons) take the boy, who, in a clash of cultural misunderstanding, murders the woman, for which crime he is lynched. As the settlers drag him to be hanged, the music box is overturned, and—in an Aristotelian recognition scene—Marty discovers that Running Wolf is actually her brother.

The painful ironies come thick and fast. William McCandless, by indulging his wife's insanity, inadvertently causes her death. The settlers, initially so eager to have their loved ones rescued, rush to judgment and kill the "formerly" white boy who, because of them, has been wrenched from the only life he knows. At the last minute, he remembers the music box (and one word of

Sgt. Posey (Andy Devine) and Lt. Gary (Richard Widmark) argue unsuccessfully with Henry Clegg (Fred Rainey).

English—"Mine, mine, mine"—significant in the climate of greed and selfishness that permeates the film), and Marty again loses her lost brother the moment she finds him.

In the end, Gary and Marty are engaged, and a now changed (or merely re-humanized) McCabe—who's been replaced in Belle's affections by his former deputy (now Marshal)—goes off with Elena to California to start anew. That each guy ends up with a gal may seem pat, but the resolution of *Two Rode Together*'s racial-prejudice plot is anything but. Nobody—not James Stewart nor the cavalry—rides to the rescue to prevent the boy's hanging. (And we neither see nor hear that the vigilantes are punished.)

The Gary-Marty and McCabe-Elena pairings (again emphasizing *two* riding together) are another instance of the movie's "doubling." In her invaluable study, *The Western Films of John Ford* (Secaucus, New Jersey: The Citadel Press, 1973), J. A. Place comments on "character doubling" in *The Searchers* and *Two Rode Together*. Just as Ethan Edwards and Chief Scar—both driven men, full of hate and out for vengeance—are two sides of the same coin, so too are McCabe and Chief Quanah Parker. (The same actor, Henry Brandon, plays both Comanche chiefs.) But they're two sides of a *different* coin: "Quanah Parker occupies about the same position in relation to McCabe that Scar did to Ethan Edwards, as a kind of alter-ego. Quanah is very different from Scar, but in much the same way McCabe is from Ethan. Quanah is greedy, practical, not entirely the leader in control of his tribe" (Place, p. 209).

Quanah Parker's name reveals his dissimilarity to *The Searchers'* antagonist. Nearly Anglo-Saxon, it's a moniker more commensurate with a merchant than the dangerous-sounding, one-syllabled *Scar*. Like McCabe, Parker is an opportunist, a pragmatist interested in the good life. He has nothing but contempt for his hotheaded, fundamentalist rival Stone Calf, who—he sneeringly tells McCabe and Gary—"still says words over buffalo shields to turn away bullets" (a piece of information McCabe uses to his advantage later in his showdown with Stone Calf, who, trusting his big medicine, walks right into the path of McCabe's bullets).

"Doubling" applies to film's heroines, too. One Indian's death provides a wrenching catharsis for Marty, in a parallel to the similar catharsis that occurs for Elena after Stone Calf is killed. Both women exorcize the "Indian" in themselves: "[Marty] tries to become the lost son for her father, even to the extent of assuming the Indian dress that he must be wearing, and adopts her brother's music box as the focal point of her obsession. Only after coming face to face with the crazed boy and witnessing his destruction is she freed from the obsession" (Place, p. 206).

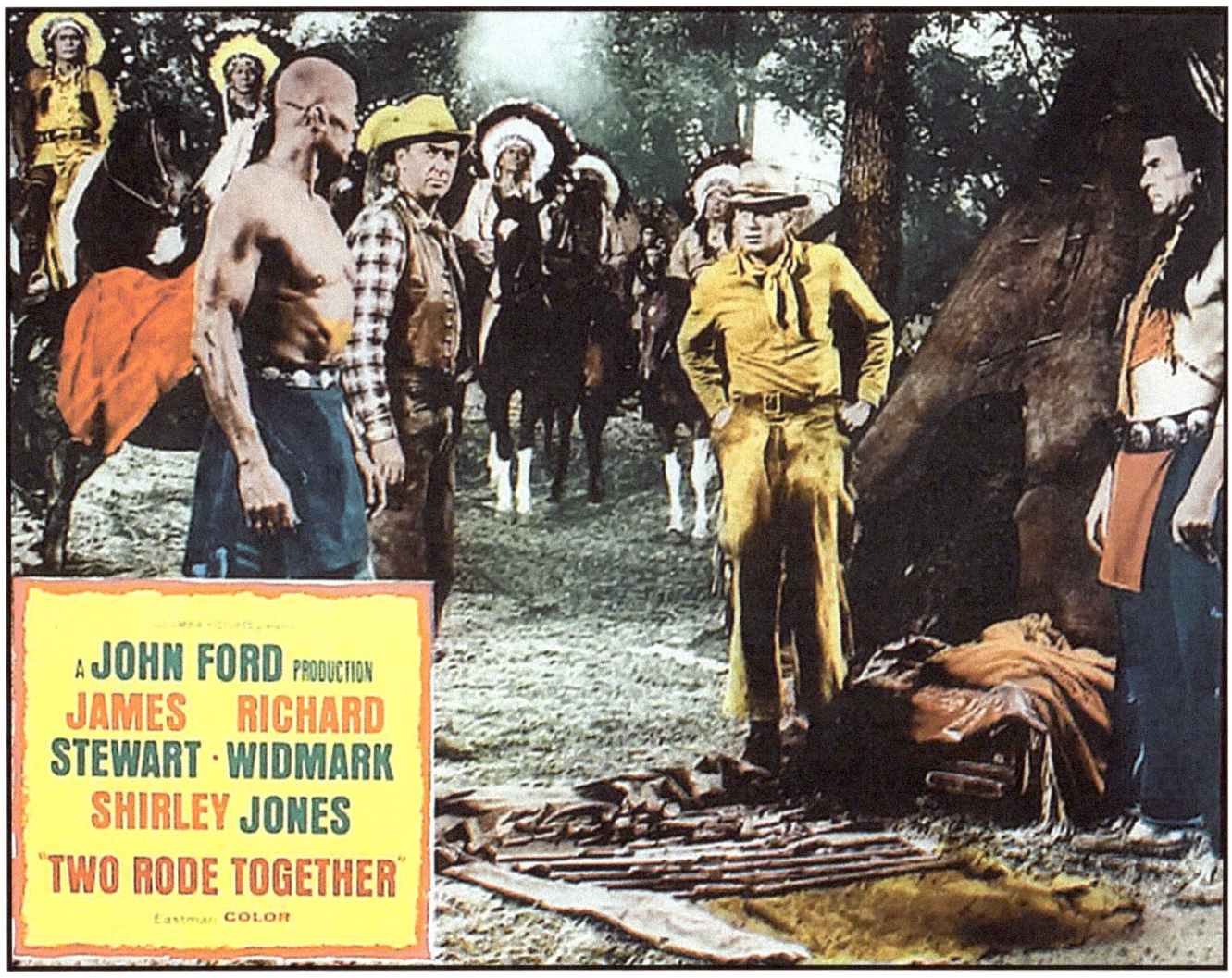
Stone Calf (Woody Strode) isn't too happy with McCabe (James Stewart) and Gary or the deal they made with Quanah Parker.

When Marty realizes the identity of the Indian being taken to his death, she wails, "Nooooo!" and throws herself to the ground. The boy is hanged; she smashes the music box to splinters and runs, crying, into Gary's arms. After McCabe shoots Stone Calf, Elena reverts to Indian mode, kneeling on the ground, keening over the fallen warrior, her husband-by-force, 'til McCabe shouts at her to stop and she runs, crying, into his arms.

For all its artful doubling, the picture suffers from some incoherent scripting. When Quanah Parker reminds McCabe that he contracted for a last captive, Elena, McCabe at first refuses—"You're gonna hafta handle Stone Calf yourself." Parker counters with "Six more rifles?" and McCabe agrees to the deal. *Why*? Because six rifles is a cheap price to pay for another prisoner? Or is Parker going to give *McCabe* the rifles?

When Parker delivers Elena to McCabe, he tells the marshal, "I'll keep the rifles," and McCabe promises to keep his side of the bargain (whatever that is): "You trust me, don't you, Quanah?"—to which the Comanche utters a resounding "No!" Other than the joke, I don't understand the gist of this conversation—although a friend, James Eliason, suggested to me that it's all a *quid pro quo*: Parker is giving McCabe his $1,000 cash cow, Running Wolf, in exchange for McCabe killing Stone Calf, who'll pursue him for Elena. If this is the intent, it's too subtle for me (and, I daresay, most viewers). McCabe does seem determined to wait for Stone Calf and have it out with him, but his pulling a gun on Gary—who wants to keep moving instead of making camp—seems poorly motivated, if at all. And the Major's later line to Gary, that, by sending Jim with McCabe, he hoped the marshal would teach Jim something the Major never could—"that only God has the right to play God"—is a total non-sequitur, a hollow-sounding "profundity" which the Machiavellian officer (who's manipulated both McCabe and his lieutenant) has a lot of nerve declaring.

Despite these infelicities, *Two Rode Together* is not the masterpiece that *The Searchers* is, but it certainly doesn't deserve the scorn heaped upon it—by its director, no less: "By the time the picture was finished, he pronounced it `the worst piece of crap I've done in 20 years,'" reports Ronald L. Davis (*John Ford: Hollywood's Old Master* [Norman, OK: University of Oklahoma Press, 1995] p. 302).

Ford's assessment was harsher than the critics' which was almost uniformly lukewarm. *Time*'s anonymous reviewer thought the "capricious, unsuccessful, but oddly likable western" showed the Master was coasting: "Director Ford's effort might

The hopeful settlers cheer on the efforts of Lt. Gary and McCabe, who promise to return kidnapped kinsmen.

be compared to the pastime of a successful gunfighter who, between important assassinations, lies on his back in a hotel room, drinks dark ale and obliterates with his six-gun all the flies on the ceiling. The onlooker admires the skill and deplores the pointlessness" ("Flies and Ale," *Time*, July 28, 1961, p. 60). "The film has validity and novelty," *Variety*'s "Tube" allowed, "but somehow...misfires" (*Variety*, June 21, 1961, p. 6). "Despite its haphazard construction," Eugene Archer called *Two Rode Together* "a compelling film" but noted that its studio had essentially "dumped" it: "Columbia...ushered the film quietly into the neighborhoods yesterday, without benefit of a Broadway opening" (*New York Times*, July 27, 1961, 23:3). By improperly promoting a movie it thought wouldn't be a hit, Columbia created a self-fulfilling prophecy. Whereas *The Searchers* was a box-office winner in 1956 (number 10, earning $4.8 million), *Two Rode Together* finished well out of the top 20.

Ford claims that he himself had little interest in the project:

> I didn't like the story, but I did it as a favor to Harry Cohn, who was stuck with the project and said, "Will you do this for me?" I said, "Good God, this is a lousy script." He said, "I know it, but we're pledged for it—we're all set—we've got Widmark and Stewart signed up." I said, "O.K., I'll do the damn thing." And I didn't enjoy it. I just tried to make Stewart's character as humorous as possible. (John Ford to Peter Bogdanovich in *John Ford* [Berkeley, California: University of California Press, 1968, rpt. 1970], pp. 97-98)

Ford certainly succeeded in making Stewart's character humorous. But does the rest of the film betray his lack of enjoyment—or was he too much of a professional to do a bad job?

Well, he didn't shoot *Two Rode Together* in Monument Valley, as he did *The Searchers*, *My Darling Clementine* (1946) and seven other pictures that were closer to his heart. But Columbia studio head Harry Cohn could be notoriously cheap—maybe Ford couldn't get the budget to film in Utah. He shot on location in southwest Texas to make use of standing sets built for John Wayne's *The Alamo* (1960; see Davis, p. 303).

The preponderance of studio sets for outdoor scenes (for some of the wagon train sequences, for the campfire scene wherein McCabe confronts and kills Stone Calf) might lead one to conclude that Ford directed *Two Rode Together* in a perfunctory manner. But false exteriors vie with the real outdoors in *The Quiet Man* (1952), *The Searchers* (most notably the campfire scene where Ethan Edwards sets a trap for and kills the traitorous trader Jerem Futterman) and in *The Man Who Shot Liberty Valance* (1962), to name just three.

Pauline Kael took Ford to task for this: "John Ford himself doesn't bother going outdoors much anymore. A few years back I dragged a painter-friend to see *The Man Who Shot Liberty Valance*; it was a John Ford Western, and though I dreaded an evening with James Stewart and John Wayne, I felt I *should* see it. My friend agreed because 'the landscapes are always great'; but after about 10 minutes of ugly studio sets, he wanted to leave" ("Saddle Sore: *El Dorado, The War Wagon, The Way West*," August 1967, reprinted in *Kiss Kiss Bang Bang* [1968; New York: Bantam, 1969], p. 53).

But all cowboy pictures aren't about vast expanses and huge vistas. Many Ford admirers (Sarris, Bogdanovich, etc.)—the same who enjoy the pictorial splendor of *Wagonmaster* (1950), *My Darling Clementine*, et al.—consider *Liberty Valance* the director's last masterpiece. Kael, who praises *Stagecoach*, doesn't allow for the "chamber Western" in her scheme of things. Just as the "chamber drama" was a play meant to be read, the "chamber Western" is an oater that could be staged. *Stagecoach* itself (like every Ford film) is character driven, and, for all its wide-open spaces, plays out in essentially narrow confines—the interior of the stagecoach and a few other locales. *The Gunfighter* (1950), *High Noon* (1952), even *Will Penney* (1968)—like *Two Rode Together* and *Liberty Valance*—are all chamber Westerns. (But that's another article.)

The scene of the hanging tree finds McCabe waving his pistol around.

Even though Ford was a pictorial director with a love of the outdoors (his first 60 films were silents and mostly Westerns), he was also a practical man who knew the control and cost-effectiveness afforded by a studio interior-as-exterior and who knew that he was creating *artifice*. In this respect, he was akin to Hitchcock, another cinema giant who often resorted to expediencies—like the sometimes painfully obvious rear projection in the motoring sequences of *Suspicion* (1941) and *Notorious* (1946). Both men were more concerned with the total effect than with the complete "realism" of individual scenes; their movies were always greater than the sum of their parts. (I prefer Ford, whose movies projected a humanity lacking in the formal experiments of Hitchcock, who was most often interested in toying with his audience than engaging their emotions—but that's also another article.)

Some might conclude that the preponderance of long takes in *Two Rode Together* indicates Ford's lack of interest in the project and desire to get it over with as quickly as possible, with the least amount of fuss. Partly because Ford made his crew wade out into the water to film Stewart and Widmark's two-shot by the river, many critics have commented on that nearly four-minute take. But, from the beginning of the film, Ford frequently shoots the two in the same frame for a sustained period of time (e.g., on the saloon's veranda when Gary comes to town; in the tent after McCabe makes his deal with Wringle)—all part of his emphasis on the *two* together of the title. Ford knew that the *motion* in motion picture doesn't always come from camera movement or quick editing or even performers' frantic antics. Sometimes the movement is in the dialogue; sometimes the motion is in the *emotion* of a scene. When two consummate actors like Stewart and Widmark play opposite each other, their conversation can drive the scene as well as any speeding stagecoach or flash pan. I doubt that many viewers are aware of—let alone bored by—the film's long takes.

Another sign of Ford's half-hearted attitude toward *Two Rode Together* could be its "almost total absence of action" ("Tube," *Variety*), which may seem strange for a Western—but not for a Ford Western, especially a post-war Ford Western, in which the characters' inner turmoil is rarely solved by moments of violence (except maybe in *The Searchers*, where, after Ethan scalps the already dead Scar—whom Martin has killed—his hate is gone, and he can take Debbie home).

That's what most of Ford's later Westerns offer—*moments* of violence. There are few action set pieces, no big shoot-outs or cavalry charges. Not that Ford could not have staged either if he wanted to (see *My Darling Clementine* and *The Searchers*), it's just that he was interested in other things. So we get a comical fistfight between Gary and the moronic Clegg brothers, Ortho (Harry Carey, Jr.) and Greely (Ken Curtis)—reminiscent of the fight between Martin and Charlie McCorry (Ken Curtis again, in a Greely-like role) in *The Searchers*, which was also a fight over a woman. (Not coincidentally, *Clegg* is the name of the villainous

Lt. Gary and Marty Purcell (Shirley Jones) are the only ones to welcome Elena (Linda Cristal), escorted by McCabe. Major Frazer (John McIntire) and others look on.

William Boyd in *Hopalong Cassidy* (1935), stunted in *The Searchers*, played bit parts in *Wagonmaster* and *Wings of Eagles* (1957) and did second-unit direction on *The Alamo*—is just awful. His McCandless has some pivotal lines, which he *cannot* deliver convincingly— and his amateurish inability is the strongest argument for Ford's dismissive attitude. Why didn't Ford hire another actor? Why didn't he hire an *actor*? But, of course, Ford was incredibly loyal and, often, created roles to include people whom he liked. Mae Marsh, Anna Lee and Jack Pennick are just three of the many performers whom Ford "made room for" in film after film. They all appear in *Two Rode Together*, and Eugene Archer singled out Marsh's cameo for thespian honors in his *New York Times* review: "The film's best acting, aside from Mr. Stewart's un-heroic sheriff [sic: marshal], comes from Mae Marsh, the large-eyed heroine of *Intolerance* and *Birth of a Nation*, as an aged captive too broken by years of suffering to return to a civilization she wistfully remembers."

Mae Marsh's role is one example of how the basic humanity and decency of Ford's characters (and world view) shine through. These traits are revealed in subtle ways, as in *The Searchers'* famous, oft-commented-upon shot where Captain Clayton (Ward Bond) studiously avoids noticing Martha Edwards (Dorothy Jordan) caress her brother-in-law's coat. In *Two Rode Together*, people lie when the truth would only hurt. When Gary finds Mrs. Clegg (Marsh) among the Comanche, and she muses about the two sons she used to have, he tells her they're grown now and that the idiot pair are "fine boys." Similarly, to protect feelings, Gary lies to Mr. Knudsen (John Quaylen) that he never found his daughter, Freda, who now has two little ones in the Comanche camp and won't leave.

Which brings us to Stewart's "un-heroic" marshal. He doesn't lie to spare feelings. He tells Marty, unkindly, some awful truths about what her brother has become if he's still alive. However, he *is* drunk at the time. He doesn't lie to Elena, either. He tells her, not unkindly, that she can't erase the memory of her years with the Comanche, that she'll carry them to her grave, but that she has to deal with them. He's *not* drunk at the time.

As mentioned earlier, *Two Rode Together* is about Guthrie McCabe regaining (reasserting) his own basic humanity and decency. He appears cynical, but of course, has a heart—witness his thinly veiled contempt when he negotiates with Wringle. However, it's a heart that can be bought—at least initially, and so he goes along with Wringle's scheme—for a price. He wants the money, but the man disgusts him, the entire misguided quest disgusts him and so he drinks—and becomes a very funny drunk (mimicking Greely Clegg's challenge to Gary to "knawk thet piece o' fahrwood off his shoulder")—until he vents his fury

family in *Wagonmaster*.) We get the split-second killing of Stone Calf over the campfire—reminiscent of Ethan's counter-ambush of Futterman in *The Searchers* (also filmed on an interior set). And we get a brief outburst of violence when the mob seizes the white Comanche teen despite Gary's futile effort to stop the lynching—which has no equivalent in *The Searchers* (although the aftermath of the cavalry's slaughter of the innocent Indians, including "Look," Martin's "wife," comes close).

Some critics complained about the picture's "inconsistency" ("Tube," *Variety*), since the tone seems to fluctuate (as evidenced by the "Laurel and Hardy" fistfight [*Time*] on the one hand and the dead-serious lynching on the other). High tragedy vies with low comedy throughout *Two Rode Together*, and this could be taken as another sign of Ford's careless handling of his material. But Shakespeare, too, alternated comedy with drama, and the fusion is common to most of Ford's films. As Place rightly remarks, "All Ford's Westerns contain an intermingling of the dramatic and the comic that enhances the emotional effect of the positive films and makes the tragedy of the darker ones more bearable. This is also true of *Two Rode Together*, which, without its comedy, would be filled with such despair that it would be unwatchable" (p. 204). She sees this as another area of comparison with *The Searchers*: "Without its rich humor, *The Searchers* would be an unbearable tragedy" (Place, p. 171).

Most of the cast is professional. Many of the performers (Carey, Jr., Curtis, Bouchey, Strode, etc.) were part of Ford's repertory company. But Cliff Lyons—who stunt-doubled for over the futility of the "rescue" mission in his thoughtless, cruel speech to Marty.

Two Rode Together was the first film James Stewart made with Ford (the other titles are *The Man Who Shot Liberty Valance*, "Flashing Spikes," an episode of the *Alcoa Premiere* TV series [broadcast 10/4/62], and *Cheyenne Autumn* [1964]). Stewart was the last of the Ford triumvirate of superstars (after Wayne and Fonda) to work for the director. He came to the Ford after a series of Anthony Mann Westerns, which re-made Stewart's image, casting him as a hard-as-nails loner, different from his pre-war Mr. Smith-type roles for Frank Capra and others. (Martin Scorsese articulates this transformation in his tribute to Stewart and Robert Mitchum, "The Men Who Knew Too Much," *Premiere*, September, 1997, pp. 70-71.) Stewart did play an unbalanced murderer early in his career: *After the Thin Man* (1936) traded on his already established persona as a nice guy to surprise the audience when he went crazy in the end. The post-war Stewart embodied *both* personae at the same time—the gangly, awkward, "aw-shucks" idealist and the angry out-for-himself survivalist. Stewart could go either way, and Ford used that tension, especially in *Two Rode Together*. The unfolding of the movie is the "softening" of Stewart's initially cynical, me-first (me-only) character.

Lt. Gary and McCabe find that Chief Quanah Parker (Henry Brandon) drives a hard bargain for the release of kidnapped settlers.

When we first view Guthrie McCabe in *Two Rode Together*, he doesn't look heroic, duded up in fancy suit and hat, yawning in a chair on the saloon porch, unconcerned about the riders who rush through the town, whooping it up, probably disturbing the peace. But there's really no doubt about his heroic stature. His costume and his easy-going self-centeredness might relate Stewart to the then popular TV character, Maverick, as embodied by James Garner. But his costume and his posture—reposing in a tilted-back chair, feet on the railing—are meant to recall for us an earlier Ford hero, Henry Fonda as Wyatt Earp in *My Darling Clementine*, who affected just such a similar attitude. In that previous film, Earp, from his porch chair, advises a gambler who's just gotten off the stagecoach to get himself some flapjacks, then get back on the stage when it leaves again in 30 minutes. Stewart's Marshal McCabe takes time from his beer and cigar to advise a couple of gamblers who've just gotten off the stagecoach to have a drink and then get back on the stage when it leaves again in *15* minutes. (The duo is surly with him until he introduces himself. Then their attitude rapidly changes to respect and fear. In *My Darling Clementine*, when Wyatt Earp utters his name, it causes a similar transformation in his auditors.) As a kind of amalgam of Fonda's marshal and his own, Stewart later played a laid-back Wyatt Earp in *Cheyenne Autumn*.

Place suggests that McCabe changes with his costumes: "When he goes out on the trail and sheds his superficial air of cynicism and hypocrisy, he also sheds the Eastern clothes and wears traditional Western dress" (p. 203). Actually, McCabe see-saws back and forth, his better instincts warring with his mercenary desires, until he takes on "seen-yore-eeta" Elena, whose doe-like dependence on her savior pulls him from the edge back onto the side of decency. The dramatic highpoint of the film, at least in terms of Stewart's character, comes when McCabe defends Elena in front of the "ladies and gentlemen" of the fort, who've been condescending and blatantly rude to her.

That McCabe's behavior here has redeemed him is illustrated by the approbation of a sympathetic supporting character. McCabe has been riling Sergeant Posey (Andy Devine) throughout the film. In the beginning, when McCabe offers to stand the soldiers to a beer, he makes his first of many cracks about Sergeant Posey's girth, and the noncom says, sarcastically, "It'll be a pleasure drinking to *your* health, Marshal." In the end, with whiskey bottle in hand, Posey listens approvingly to McCabe's tirade on behalf of Elena, then he *does* drink, happily, sincerely, to the Marshal's health.

The final irony of *Two Rode Together* is that McCabe, who undertook a rescue mission which he considered fruitless just to get away from a woman hankering to marry him, actually achieves the salvation of one captive, Elena, whom he ends up wanting to marry (or at least to ride off into the sunset with). Jim Gary underscores the completion of McCabe's journey from partial morality to whole man in the film's last line: "I guess old Guth found something he wanted more than 10 percent of."

Two Rode Together, like *The Searchers*, *She Wore a Yellow Ribbon* (1949) and all of Ford's post-war Westerns, respects the inherent dignity of the Indians. Ford is never condescending to America's First Immigrants; he never treats them as cardboard villains. (*Cheyenne Autumn*, his penultimate picture, elevates them to the level of protagonists.) When we watch *Two Rode Together* (or *The Searchers*), we grant the movie our willing suspension of disbelief and do not question the basic premise—the veracity of the captivity narrative—did Indians ever really kidnap white women and children (and how often), or is it one of those folk stories colonialists like to spread about groups they've enslaved or exterminated, in order to justify their own reprehensible, immoral behavior? But that's another article.

MAD ABOUT MOVIES DVD REVIEWS

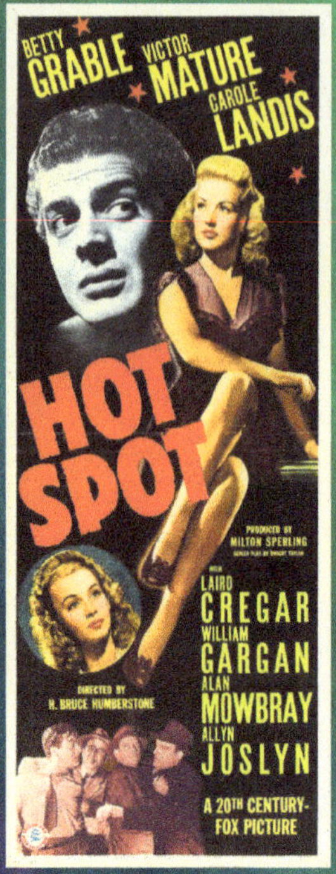

by Gary J. Svehla

Ratings: Excellent 4; Good 3; Fair 2; Poor 1

I Wake Up Screaming
Movie: 3.5; Disc: 4.0
[Fox]

Fox Film Noir regularly released two or three titles every three months or so (until 2008), and while some of the so-called films noir are borderline, all are exceptional and have been providing plenty of entertainment at affordable pricing. *I Wake Up Screaming*, released in 1941 (it was to have been released as *Hot Spot*, but the title was changed at the last moment) and directed by H. Bruce Humerstone, is the perfect example of why the Fox DVD film noir series is so essential. First of all we have all the noir icons present: Victor Mature playing Frankie, a sports promoter, who views beautiful women as commodities to be marketed; Carole Landis as Vicky, the hash slinger who becomes a beautiful fashion model that is mysteriously murdered; Betty Grable as Vicky's sister Jill, who at first disapproves of Frankie's methods but slowly falls in love with him; Laird Cregar as hulking police inspector Cornell, the watchdog who hounds Frankie, claiming he won't put the cuffs around him until he has the goods to get him fried; Elisha Cook, Jr. as Harry, the apartment telephone operator that is obsessed with Vicky. All these characterizations are enacted deftly.

I Wake Up Screaming is a character study, but one that is filmed exquisitely in all the shades of black necessary to create a haunting mental portrayal that delves the depths of evil in the human soul. Frankie is a hustler, a promoter, a person who introduces naïve young girls to all the right people in hope that he can jumpstart their career and make a hefty profit acting as promoter. He is an Italian that rose from the streets, a man who remembers the old neighborhood but also knows that he does not want to fall back down into that poor lifestyle again. Vicky to him is a beautiful woman, but a woman with whom he enjoys a warm yet professional relationship, escorting her to all the trendy nightspots, but without getting personally involved. Once Vicky is killed in her apartment, the quietly intense police inspector Cornell is convinced that Frankie did her in and he works slowly but methodically to tighten the noose around his neck (in one interesting sequence, Cornell asks Frankie to give him a lift home, all the while he ties a noose with a piece of twine, the finished symbol left on the car seat as he exits). Cornell, a well-groomed man, who weighs close to 300 pounds, never raises his voice, seldom becomes angry and always punctuates his threats with humor. Along with *The Lodger*, this movie features Cregar's finest performance. And Betty Grable, usually associated for her WW II leggy pinup posters and her Fox movie musicals, plays the beautiful girl next door who works a 9-to-5 job and lives in the shadow of her more flamboyant sister, who craves the limelight and stardom. Jill seems fascinated with the man that exploited her sister and fueled her fantasy obsessions, but as she gets to know the real Frankie underneath, she cannot help but fall in love with him.

Featuring a story that is equal parts crime drama, mystery, thriller and romance, *I Wake Up Screaming* entertains because the bevy of interesting, eccentric characters developed within the mystery constantly suck the audience into the deeply muted noir tones created by cinematographer Edward Cronjager, his visual universe of ambivalent morality becoming the heart of film noir.

For once Fox has pulled out all the stops for the supplementals. Besides the usual audio commentary, production and photo gallery and trailers, the DVD contains one deleted sequence involving Betty Grable as well as the original opening title and poster art, when the film was called *Hot Spot* and not *I Wake Up Screaming*. The bottom line is that this is one of the better noir titles released and it again shows that no one does film noir better than 20th Century Fox.

Vicki
Movie: 2.5; Disc: 3.5
[Warner]

Twelve years after Fox released *I Wake Up Screaming*, director Harry Horner returned to the same well in 1953 for *Vicki*, a virtual remake of the superior, earlier noir. While both films are told partially in flashback, *Vicki* depends even more on such a frame, and while the stories and even some of the dialogue is identical, *Vicki* fails to resonate. Mostly it may be the second-tier cast that produces inferior results; however, Richard Boone as Cornell is not bad, although the more-subtle Laird Cregar shines even brighter. For instance, Cregar, a big mass of a man, intimidates with his size but his line delivery is often low key, intense and arrogant in a quiet manner. Boone's Cornell is brooding and bone weary. The film starts with Cornell checking into a quiet hotel, out in the boonies, to sleep for a week, this being his vacation. But when he sees the headlines that model Vicki Lynn has been murdered, he phones his office immediately and demands that the case be given to him. Boone tends to always be deep in thought and he sometimes delivers his dialogue in almost a whisper, but then rage explodes from within and he erupts with a burst of screaming demands. The disparity between the quiet, internal intensity and his emotional outbursts only cue the viewer that this detective is disturbed, something that Cregar was able to disguise in the original. Boone's performance is solid, but Cregar's is inspired.

The sister act of ambitious Vicki Lynn (Jean Peters) and more sensible Jill Lynn (Jeanne Crain) in *Vicki* does not hit the heights of the former duo of Vicky (Carole Landis) and Jill (Betty Grable). While Jean Peters projects the right amount of arrogance and ambition, she tends to come off as the harder-edged character, compared to Carole Landis' performance. When Peters announces to boy friend/PR manager Steve Christopher (Elliott Reid) that she is Hollywood bound, she is abrupt, unthankful and very self-serving. She seems cold, a ruthless young waitress that is almost using Christopher. She leaves him saddled with contracts that he signed to help her career. Carole Landis seems far less ruthless and a tad more grateful, and the audience can hold more sympathy for the character in the earlier movie. Betty Grable as the less starry-eyed sister was very perky and sensual in the original production, and slowly comes to fall in love with Christopher (who in the guise of Victor Mature is more sizzle and sex than

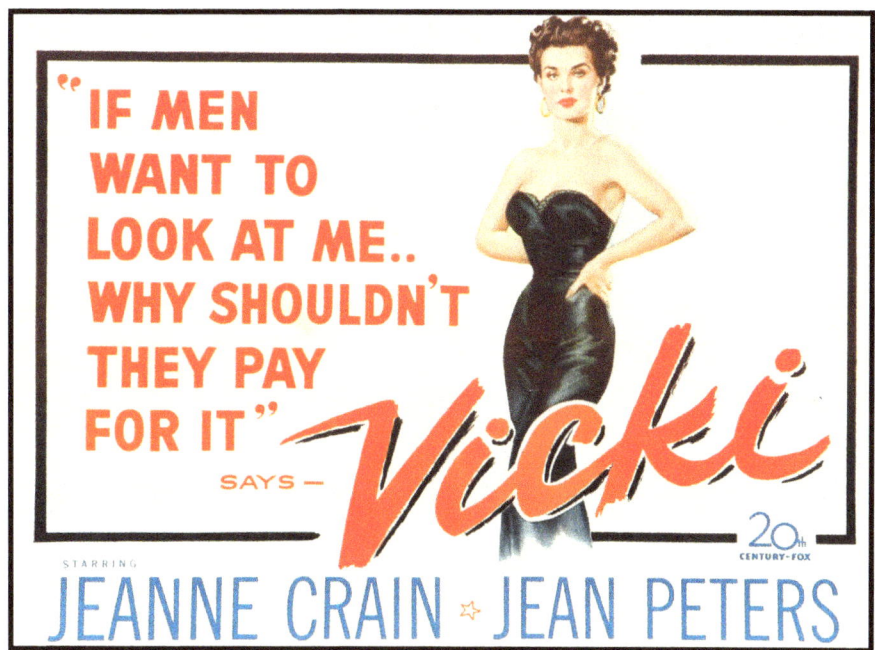

the more proper and polite Elliott Reid) in a realistic manner. Jeanne Crain plays a pretty Jill, yet her character has far less charisma and spark when compared to Grable's performance. Yes, Jill and Christopher do fall in love, but their characters are not very romantic and the relationship that builds is far less exciting.

Beyond performances, *Vicki* only shines in the film's opening and closing sequences. When the film begins, we have a panoramic night view of the city with Vicki's face plastered over billboards and posters that are everywhere to be seen. Her sensuous cool but sizzling face is soon contrasted to the view of her foot sticking out of the sheet, as a stretcher carrying her corpse is taken from her apartment. And at the film's conclusion, we watch as a man pastes a new poster over the slightly fading one of Vicki, demonstrating just how deposable fashion models can be. The rest of the film appears low-rent compared to the 1941 original. The little restaurant where Vicky works in the original is expansive with plenty of glass to allow Cornell to leer spookily in at her from the outside. In the remake the restaurant is tiny and does not seem to be as easily penetrated from stalkers standing outside. The art direction is far less interesting, and while the nightclub sequences are fine, the cinematography just seems more pedestrian with less distinctive visual style. The interrogation sequences are nicely bathed in shades of black, but again they come up short.

And *Vicki*, rather than being a rethinking of the original, is more a direct remake only reminding the viewer how much better the earlier film was. And only 12 years earlier at that! If *I Wake Up Screaming* had never been made, *Vicki* would shine that much brighter, being the very first screen version of the Steve Fisher novel. But rather than go back to the original source, *Vicki* goes back only to the original movie and reminds us why *I Wake Up Screaming* is an excellent film noir.

Force of Evil
Movie: 3.0; Disc: 3.0
[Republic/Lions Gate]

Some film noirs are better at expressing their philosophy than for providing entertainment value, and *Force of Evil* just happens to be one of those productions. The movie itself is excellently made, featuring fine acting from John Garfield as Joe and Thomas Gomez as his brother Leo, with Paul Fix playing violent criminal Ficco. However, here the screenplay is the star and never has the morally ambivalent world of film noir been so well defined.

The movie involves the numbers racket and the criminal syndicate that controls the money. Joe Moss is a former Wall Street lawyer, who is working for the syndicate kingpin Ben Tucker (Roy Roberts). Joe is mainly responsible for eliminating the gun play, the dead bodies and the mayhem from the mob, and he has a plan to bankrupt all the individual racket "banks" by having a specific number hit on July 4. Then Tucker can move in and offer all the little banks loans as long as they align themselves with him and transform themselves from individually run "banks" into one large corporate one. In

his mind Ben sees a million dollar pay off, and making money is his sole purpose in life.

However, in his mind brother Leo is a respectable businessman. Even though his business, the numbers racket, is a criminal enterprise, he treats all his clients honestly and equally. Leo wants to quit the racket rather than merge with all the other banks and become controlled totally by the mob. Joe tells Leo to leave, to get out tonight, before the July 4th fireworks, where the bottom will fall out. Leo tells him his clients invested their hard-earned money, and he considers it a debt, one that he has to follow through on. Integrity is how Leo lives his life and brother Joe just does not understand such a philosophy in such a corrupt business. When Joe pleads with his brother to go in with Tucker's syndicate, the heavyset man, who has a bad heart, gets blue in the face and screams, "I am sensible. I am calm. I'll give you my answer calmly and sensibly, my final answer. My final answer is finally no. The answer is no! Absolutely and finally no! Finally and positively no! No! No! No!!!" Joe even has the police raid his brother's operation to apply some heat, but an innocent office worker gets arrested and now has a police record. Leo asks Joe to help set her up in a legitimate office job. The girl Doris (Beatrice Pearson) is taciturn and non-emotional, yet she slowly falls in love with the flawed lawyer Joe. She becomes his moral conscience and the voice of good within him. But by the movie's end Tucker, becoming frustrated with Joe's non-violent methods, brings in loose canon Ficco to pressure the individual numbers banks to stay in the business and fall in line. Unfortunately Leo is carted out of a restaurant forcefully and killed, his body left battered and broken on the rocks underneath a bridge. Joe sees that Tucker is forcing him out by moving Ficco in, and the film's climax deals with Joe's revenge and attempt to survive this gangland powerplay.

The moral ambiguity is front and center. Joe is devoted to his business with the mob, but he also loves and respects his stubborn brother Leo, whom he tries to protect. Doris is the young innocent, slightly tainted, but a woman who can make Joe feel the guilt of his immoral life. At the same time, Joe is scheming against his brother's racket operation to have him busted by the police, until he sees the virtue of joining Tucker's larger syndicate. Leo, of course, is stubborn and holds fast to his morals. But at the same time the bookkeeper within Leo's operation is working with the police as an informer, to bring down the entire operation. So we have two different people with two entirely different motives attempting the same goal—destroy Leo's old-school numbers racket by any means necessary.

By the movie's end the universe has been turned topsy-turvey, in a startling and abrupt ending, with both Ficco and Tucker dead, Leo dead, and Doris and Joe left alive to attempt to pick up the pieces of their lives as the end credits roll.

Force of Evil, featuring assured direction from Abraham Polonsky (also co-writer), with wonderful shadowy noir photography from George Barnes, creates a smoky world of the city's underdogs, people that attempt to get by and still preserve their dignity and integrity by any means possible. *Force of Evil* is an apt title, but it is also a movie that is dreary, depressed, unhappy and ultimately existing in a universe lacking hope. The message is visceral like a punch to the gut and apparently no winners exist, only those crafty enough to survive.

Nightmare Alley
Movie: 3.0; Disc: 3.5
[Fox]

Nightmare Alley became a cult film by nature of its lack of availability on home video for so many years. This A-budgeted film noir, starring Tyrone Power, is unlike any other film noir ever produced, and opening in 1947, it was riding the noir wave of then current popularity. The screenplay by Jules Furthman and direction by Edmund Goulding is equally eccentric, making this film one of the most off-putting noirs ever produced.

Power stars as Stanton Carlisle, a drifter, who becomes involved in the carnival world, saying for the first time he has something that means more than just a job, that as a carny he feels superior to the bumpkins he cons. Stan, as he is called, is ambitious, self-centered and greedy, and he attaches himself to Zeena (Joan Blondell), with whom he has an affair. Zeena is devoted to her alcoholic husband Frank (Ian Keith), a man that made it to the top, but now is a broken shell of former greatness. Stan wants to find the fame and popularity that Frank had achieved. He sees his opportunity in learning "the code," or language by which carny mentalists can communicate with one another. In the act, Zeena is perched atop her wagon while Frank, too drunk to perform the bit as it should be done, hides beneath the floor and can literally write notes to Zeena about things people in the audience hold up and expect Zeena to name. However, if he knows the code, Stan can go out into the audience, and by his voice inflection, let Zeena know the object that people are holding or thinking about. Zeena knows how secretive the code is and she is very cautious about sharing it. In a fatalistic course of events, Stan accidentally, in an act of kindness, gives Frank his own bottle of gin, but mistakenly it turns out to be rubbing alcohol and Frank dies. Stan, even though having a sexual relationship with Zeena, liked Frank and wanted to be kind to him, so his responsibility in the man's death haunts and damages the manipulative Stan.

shadow or long shot, other times when a barker throws two chickens on stage. In the carny world, the geek is the lowest of the low, a man who has hit rock bottom and is willing to be degraded nightly for cheap booze and a little money. Typically the geek is an alcoholic (like Frank) and prone to throwing fits and running amok. Stan asks, how could a man get that low. But by the film's final act, Stan, damaged and fast becoming an alcoholic, gives his final $150 to Molly and sends her home. As could be predicted from the first act, at the movie's end, Stan has hit rock bottom, becomes a disheveled drunk and accepts the job as the carny geek, having risen too fast and fallen too hard.

Nightmare Alley's acting is uniformly first-rate, with Tyrone Power's eccentric against-type performance the standout of the film and one of the best performances of his career (which was usually filled with romantic leading man roles). While Stanton was always self-centered and greedy, he was also kind, ambitious and likeable. At first haunted by his guilt over the death of his mentor, whose secret code he secretly coveted, Stanton's descent into mental collapse is tragic in the Greek sense, as his lust for fame makes him vulnerable and an easy mark for the cold-blooded Lilith. By the movie's last sequence, when Molly finds the pathetic wreck that Stanton becomes, the hope exists for redemption and thus the film's noir glumness is somewhat dissipated.

Nightmare Alley is a dark and unsettling morality play where Frank's rise and fall, wonderfully played by the underrated Ian Keith, becomes a warning to underling Stanton of the pitfalls to avoid in the carny world. And when Stanton becomes the drunken geek, losing every ounce of self-respect, the audience understands that Stanton has fallen even lower than the equally sympathetic Frank. The superb direction by Edmund Goulding allows the audience to foresee this tragedy from the very first sequence, which focuses on the drunken geek, and that symbol becomes the film's dominant image. *Nightmare Alley* was long overdue for DVD release and the presentation here makes it a noir to study and appreciate…and perhaps even enjoy.

Sorry, Wrong Number
Movie: 3.0; Disc: 3.5
[Columbia]

By 1948 Hollywood mainstream was pretty much at its artistic peak recreating suspense cinema of the darkest noir tone. Lucile Fletcher expanded and adapted her famous radio play *Sorry, Wrong Number* for the Hollywood screen, and while the plot becomes slightly convoluted and excessive in the translation, the story is superbly suspenseful. The cast, headed by Barbara Stanwyck (in her Academy Award-nominated performance) and supported by talent such as Burt Lancaster, Ed Begley, Harold Vermilyea, Ann Richards and others, drives the suspense to dizzyingly heights.

The movie never gets better than when the camera lingers in the bedroom of Leona (Stanwyck) at the movie's beginning and end. Here the cinematography becomes the real star of the show, with the type of subjective camera point-of-view perspective made famous by John Carpenter and others 30 years later, and pulls the viewer in with its subtlety. Leona, a rich and lonely invalid, finds herself totally alone in her bedroom located at the top of a spiraling staircase. In the movie's first minutes, she overhears two men plotting to murder a woman, and Leona, shocked and scared, notifies the police, who simply are not interested in helping until a crime occurs. The film begins as the audience snakes its way through a deserted office at night, ending up at the desk of husband Henry (Lancaster), whose phone receiver lies on the desk, disconnected. As

the frantic Leona tries desperately to reach her husband, who promised to be home, she looks outside her huge bay window which overlooks the harbor. As the frightened, helpless woman looks around her bedroom, we see all the tables with pills, and the door leading to the staircase that winds downward and downward, every shot bathed in shadows and darkness. The movie's opening shows a switchboard operator plugging wires in and out of the board. For invalid Leona, a telephone network becomes her lifeline, and the movie's plot is revealed, both in the present and in flashback, by a series of phone calls she makes to various people trying to locate her husband.

By piecing together all the diverse, disconnected sequences, the audience learns that Leona steals the hulk Henry away from Sally (Ann Richards), the girl that Henry had been dating. Leona's wealthy father owns a drug corporation, and by accepting a marriage proposal from Leona, Henry (who is working class from a small out-of-the-way burg) will be set up as vice-president. The ambitious man quickly marries Leona, and her father (Begley) does make Henry a vice president, but in title only. Henry becomes king of the five-copy invoices for the corporation, stifling his creative needs. After being out of Henry's life for eight years, Sally re-enters when she discovers that her attorney husband, who does special cases for the District Attorney, is following a lead on Henry, whose nefarious enterprises involve a milquetoast Brit named Evans and a deserted beach house on Staten Island. Things come to a head when the beach house is torched and Sally discovers a link with Leona's father's company. By this point Leona is reduced to screaming and panicking each time the phone rings, and all the shadows surrounding her bedroom become ominous and threatening. Further events prove that Leona is not actually ill at all; her physical problems exist only in her mind.

It seems Henry and the corporation's chemist Evans have gone into private business with a certain mobster Morano, and after finding financial success, Henry decides to cut Morano out. Of course Morano discovers the deception and demands that Henry and Evans pay $200,000 or die. Ironically the police apprehend Morano, but Henry, having passed the deadline date to pay off his debt, is forced to hire murderers to kill Leona for her insurance money, to pay off the mob. So in the film's final minutes, Leona, frantic, tries to phone for help as a shadowy figure enters the house, via an open window, and starts to advance toward the staircase. Finally Henry reaches Leona over the phone, and he tells his wife she has three minutes to live, that she must get out of the bed and escape…as the killer enters the bedroom and Leona screams.

Sorry, Wrong Number does a fabulous job of recounting a complex plot piecemeal, the pieces of the jigsaw puzzle are revealed out of chronological order in a most clever and suspenseful manner. Even though Henry need not have had his wife killed for the mob money since Morano was arrested, by the time he discovers the truth the wheels have been put in motion, and everyone at this point in time is doomed by fate. Director Anatole Litvak keeps the suspense building and building until the climax explodes in the film's final minutes. A wonderful marriage of the printed page and cinema, *Sorry, Wrong Number* becomes a suspense classic that features a terrific Barbara Stanwyck performance.

Warner Oland is Charlie Chan Vol. 1
Movies: *Charlie Chan in London* (2.5); *Charlie Chan in Paris* (3.0); *Charlie Chan in Shanghai* (2.5); *Charlie Chan in Egypt* (3.0); Discs: 3.5 [Fox]

After the *Chanology* box set documented several of the Monogram-produced Sydney Toler 1940s Charlie Chan movies, it is a pleasant surprise to see the earlier 20th CenturyFox Chan films, starring Warner Oland, released to home video, chronologically. Even though only four features are included in this box set, the entire Charlie Chan Fox series was eventually released, with stunning restoration.

The problem with these early Warner Oland releases (all debuted in 1934 or 1935) is that the original source material is good, if not exceptional. The films appear to be grainy and sometimes the contrast is not as well defined as we might hope. The soundtracks are not as booming as one might expect. Of course audiences must consider that at least some of these moves were presumed lost, so finding them on DVD is cause to celebrate. These Chans feature screenplays *based* upon the character created by Earl Diggs Bigger, so few of the actual novels have actually been filmed. And the problem with mysteries made in the mid-1930s Hollywood is that what was once considered original and startling is now cliché and old hat. Even so, the mystery plots hold up quite well and keep audiences guessing.

The oldest movie in this box set is *Charlie Chan in London*, co-starring "Raymond" Milland, perhaps the creakiest production in the set, and the plot is the easiest one to figure out, with very few true surprises or thrills. Keye Luke as Lee Chan will not be introduced until the next movie in the series, so the humor is kept to a minimum, a real shame. The manor house settings and the dank mood create the most interest here, but the plot is fairly standard and the mystery, even with a screenplay by Philip MacDonald, is too obvious. Of course it is the character of Charlie Chan, as created by Warner Oland, that provides the most interest for viewers here, and

A Swedish poster for *Charlie Chan in Shanghai*

while further entries will better establish his nuances and quirks, Oland's Chan is shown immediately as extraordinarily polite and self-depreciating but always sporting that all-knowing twinkle in his eye. And, while he is a man of few words, his quiet wisdom radiates. Fortunately, the series got better over time and *Charlie Chan in London* is still worth revisiting.

The second film, *Charlie Chan in Paris*, is one of the best of the set. Philip MacDonald's story is fleshed out with other writers and the plot is quite clever and it is nearly impossible to predict whodunit until the closing moments. The studio-created mood of Paris is very well defined, especially the opening sequence in a café where undercover agent Nardi (Dorothy Appleby) does an Apache dance with a partner (the stereotypical Parisian dance where the male dancer, usually a gangster, throws the sexy female all over the dance floor), and during the dance's thrilling conclusion, the male tosses Nardi through a stage window, where she crashes safely. However, a mysterious knife-wielding figure in the shadows kills Nardi, and he vanishes quickly as Chan runs to hear her cryptic final words. Such thrills and expense were missing from *Charlie Chan in London*, with *In Paris* the series is surefooted. As mentioned, Keye Lucke enters the series as enthusiastic Number One Son Lee Chan, playing the energetic pup to the wizened "Pop" Chan. Their relationship and warmth becomes a cornerstone of the series, and also at the same time a sense of humor is able to be added to the formula, without aberrant shifts in tone. The plot involves forged bank bonds and a mysterious crippled, gruff Parisian, who always turns up directly before or after murders occur, and it becomes apparent that this man, whose features are well hidden by gloves, large dark glasses and floppy hats, is the murderer in disguise. But the twist becomes even more convoluted than this. Sporting an involving and thrilling plot and well-honed red herrings, *Charlie Chan in Paris* ups the ante and becomes most entertaining.

Next up is *Charlie Chan in Egypt*, and once again the studio sets substitute nicely for the Egyptian landscape, and the film features some creepy sequences of grisly horror, with a missing scientist found dead within a sarcophagus and wrapped as an ancient mummy. Other moody sequences include underground caverns within the excavation site, with hidden passageways and lurking danger. The mysterious opening sequence, showing the unveiling of the Egyptian tomb, is worthy of any Universal Pictures Mummy movie. And during the climax, several tunnel sequences, illuminated by lantern light, are truly worthy of any horror movie. In contrast to the superb comic support provided by Mantan Moreland in the Monogram Sydney Toler Chans, we have a racially stereotyped one-note caricature provided by Stephin Fletchit as Snowshoes. *Charlie Chan in Egypt* features interesting death sequences, including the earlier corpse in a sarcophagus sequence. Later the professor's son is killed quite cleverly as he plays his violin and strikes a chord that breaks a vial of poison gas inside the instrument. Another fine bit has our leading man Tom (Thomas Beck) swim underwater, in flooded Egyptian tombs, and surface in the treasure cave, where the unseen murderer strikes again by firing two shots into Tom's chest. Even the sexy Rita Hayworth (billed as Rita Cansino) plays a mysterious house servant, who knows more than she is willing to say. *Charlie Chan in Egypt* features moody cinematography, horrific set pieces and cleverly staged deaths and a complex plot that is totally involving.

Lastly, we have *Charlie Chan in Shanghai*, perhaps the second weakest entry, but one still yards ahead of the first *Charlie Chan in London*. The movie once again attempts to create an international ethnic favor, but the budget limits the production, photographed on studiobound sets. The movie starts out promisingly as Charlie Chan is on a ship bound for Shanghai, China to attend a banquet honoring him for his humble efforts. It just so happens that at the same time son Lee is sent by his company to Shanghai, so if the plot drags a tad, we are entertained by the father-son relationship and the resulting humorous antics. At the

banquet Charlie's friend Sir Stanley reveals he discovered some interesting news, which delayed him, and as he presents a special ornate jade box to Charlie, a booby-trapped pistol inside fires, killing Sir Stanley instantly, thus instigating the caper that will drive the narrative. The film's best sequences involve the mysterious gang that is trying to kill Chan and the clever means by which they attempt to snare the clever detective, including placing one of their members as the hotel operator, who reports all information directly to the gang. In one thrilling sequence, Chan receives a visit from the police commissioner's representative, who states that a car is waiting to take him directly to see the commissioner. Of course Chan checks out the message by phoning the commissioner, but the nefarious hotel operator patches him through to the gangsters, one of whom pretends to be the head cop. Chan leaves to meet the car, when the real commissioner phones Chan's room and tells son Lee that he did not ask to see his father. Of course this leads to Lee Chan getting into a taxi to follow the gangsters and save his father. Such stunts become the high point of the production and make this another entertaining Chan entry.

Bonus features in this box set include excellent documentaries, but the real treat is the inclusion of *Eran Trece*, the Spanish language version of the lost and first talkie Chan mystery, released as *Charlie Chan Carries On*. In *Eran Trece* Manuel Arbo plays Chan. While the better Chan entries await, this first volume offers plenty of entertainment and whets the appetite for more.

Charlie Chan Collection Vol. 2
Movies: *Charlie Chan at the Circus* (2.5); *Charlie Chan at the Race Track* (2.5); *Charlie Chan at the Opera* (3.0); *Charlie Chan at the Olympics* (2.5); Disc: 3.5 [Warner Bros.]

After the appearance of one box set of Monogram Syndey Toler-released Charlie Chan features and the first boxed set of the earliest Warner Oland released Chans, it is delightful to see Warner Bros. carry-on with the latest collection (four movies total, all released in 1936-1937) of Warner Oland Chans. And since these productions are all mid-1930s releases, the print quality and sound is superior to the first collection.

With the Charlie Chan series, viewers are getting a formulaic B-series of mysteries based upon a pulp literary detective. Warner Bros. never intended any of the Chan entries to be high art. Instead each entry in the series becomes light movie fare, whose only purpose is to entertain, and entertain these movies do. Some a little better than others, but all of the Chans are lively early morning entertainment, each movie lasting little over an hour.

First up is *Charlie Chan at the Circus*, the first movie in the series to show the entire Chan family (including Mrs. Chan), who are special guests at the circus. All the children, from youngest to oldest, move in synchronized motion, lining up at their seats but not sitting down until their father sits first. The mystery and murder is strictly by the book, with the new circus co-owner Joe Kinney (who comes from a surly background of managing honky tonks) molded as a jerk, providing reasons why he might be killed in the movie's first minutes. He is about to marry, and his jilted lover swears revenge, as does her new male companion. The former sole owner of the circus, John Gaines, needed capital to bail out the circus, and Kinney was the man available. Now Kinney threatens to take over the show if Gaines is too slow to pay him back. Kinney is very cruel with the animals and lacks sensitivity, which makes the animal handlers hate him and threaten to quit. The list goes on and on, so when all these people are gathered together and the key to the gorilla cage is dropped, one sneaky hand bends over and grabs the key,

which becomes important in the forthcoming murder of Kinney. In another classic mystery ploy, the murder occurs in a locked room, in this case the circus business wagon. The room is locked from the inside with only a sunroof on top allowing access. Chan uses Colonel Tim (a "little" person) and the circus giant to gain access to the room, and inside Tim finds Kinney dead. At key points in the story the circus ape escapes and runs amok, and when it is discovered that Kinney's neck has been snapped, the assumption is that the escaped ape is the murderer.

Of course things are never as simple as they look, and when a quick glance lists the name of J. Carrol Naish in the credits, one is aware immediately that Naish typically plays the villain, so all eyes are now on him. And by the film's end, the original assumption that both the ape and Naish are the killers just may turn out to be true. But enough said there. Keye Luke as Lee Chan becomes an indispensable component of the B series and the juxtaposing of old Chinese ways and evolving Americanized Chinese attitudes always adds life to the proceedings.

The second production in the collection is *Charlie Chan at the Race Track*, a film that is slightly inferior to the first entry by nature of its less colorful centerpiece. Let's face it, the circus lends itself to mystery and intrigue with its carny atmosphere of citizens who exist on the outskirts of the law. Add contorted ladies, little people and giants and we have a odd cast of characters. Then add wild escaped apes and we have a high quotient of suspense and thrills. The racetrack, while populated by seedy people, gamblers and the very wealthy, also lends itself to a good mystery. However, only the beginning and the ending of this Chan entry occur at the racetrack. The majority of the film occurs onboard a cruise ship transporting two horses from Europe to America, for their first race together. Shipboard is a too familiar setting for the Chan series and before long an air of sameness settles in.

Surprisingly the murder occurs off screen and is revealed via a letter that mentions the death of the owner of the winning racehorse. It seems the owner was kicked to death by his horse in the shipboard stable stall. The monkey owned by Streamline Jones (John Henry Allen) supposedly spooked the horse and caused the animal to kill its owner. However, by the spray of the blood, Chan knows that the horse was not the murderer. The suspects include members of the immediate family, the owners of the rival horse and members of the crooked gambling syndicate that controls racetrack betting. To be quite honest, the mystery becomes

lethargic and of little interest by itself. What brings this entry to livid life is the expanded participation of Keye Luke as Lee, Chan's son, whose participation leads to suspense and laughter throughout. Forbidden by his father to take the sea voyage with him, Lee gets hired on as a steward, but in the course of investigating private rooms, his boss ends up chasing Lee around the ship and finally, with Charlie's approval, throws the boy into the brig for the remainder of the sea voyage (which thankfully ends at this moment).

The film's climax is exciting, involving the substituting of one horse for the other, so the gamblers can make tons of money in one race. Just in case the wrong horse gets into the lead, the gangsters have a device ready that shoots a dart into any horse that gets in the way. While the gamblers are early-on revealed as the criminals, their major boss is a mystery figure revealed during the film's final moments. And here is the surprise expected at the end of every Chan entry. This one does not disappoint.

Next is *Charlie Chan at the Opera*, the Chan that many people consider one of the best, if for no other reason than the inclusion of co-star Boris Karloff and the expensive opera sets employed, giving the production a B+ look of extravagance. The opera sets were left over from another movie *Metropolitan*, made a year earlier, so director H. Bruce Humberstone was taking advantage of still standing sets.

Because of the co-starring status of Boris Karloff (his opening sequence in a sanatorium, where he has been confined for the past seven years, starts the movie off in a most dramatic way), Keye Luke's participation, so essential to the success of the last film, is here greatly reduced. Luke's sequences are limited to his theatrical disguises, playing an armor-wearing soldier in an entire regiment of such soldiers. Once in a while Lee Chan will see a trap door open and close and then take a detour down below to acquire a piece of evidence. Such sequences are suspenseful and hilarious at the same time, but his lack of screen time is sorely felt.

The presence of icon horror star Boris Karloff is a real boon for the production, and Karloff's sad face and obsession to be reunited with his daughter adds dramatic weight to an otherwise tried and true mystery formula. Karloff seems to inhabit every nook and hidden cranny of the Gothic opera house, making him a virtual phantom of the opera. Easily slipping into costume disguises and thus able to mimic the appearance of performers in the opera, Karloff is able to appear and disappear at will. Of course Karloff is the red herring. For instance, in one on-stage dramatic sequence, Karloff dons the costume of male lead Borelli (Gregory Gaye) and performs his part on stage, culminating with the knifing of his former wife Madame Rochelle (Margaret Irving). The movie audience suspects Karloff's Gravelle actually stabbed the woman, but in reality, she is actually only unconscious, while the actual murder occurred only after she was brought back to her dressing room. When Borelli, Madame

Rochelle's lover, is also killed, all fingers point to jilted Gravelle, whom Rochelle and Borelli conspired to murder all these years ago. Of course, in the universe of Charlie Chan, such assumptions usually fail to hold any credence and the actual killer is revealed in the movie's final minutes.

Charlie Chan at the Opera is definitely one of the better entries, with the stand-out sympathetic performance of star Karloff, and the opera's hidden corridors, secret passageways and creepy basement all add an aura of horror and suspense that only enhances the mystery, which is aided by an effective plot.

The final film in the set, *Charlie Chan at the Olympics* (1937), was again directed by H. Bruce Humberstone and featured more suspense in the whodunit arena. The story is spy oriented involving a newly designed airplane that can be remote controlled. Its inventors wanted to create this new weapon for the United States, but during its initial test run the pilot is murdered and a stowaway assassin takes control of the plane, crash lands it and steals the controlling device. Charlie Chan's job is to recover the new scientific technology before it falls into enemy hands, and the case takes Charlie and Lee Chan to Berlin, where Lee will compete on the United States swim team. Of course Olympic footage of Jesse Owen running is interwoven into the plot.

For once, the plot is a tad too convoluted, involving the inventors who may not be as pro-American as they first appear, a gentleman bandit named Hughes, who has been trying to acquire the aircraft controller for some time and a man named Zaraka, who heads a spy network throughout Europe. A mysterious femme fatale character, Yvonne Roland, and her allegiance may fall on either side of the fence. Of course, just when audiences believe they have the mystery figured out, Charlie Chan demonstrates that resolutions to complex crimes are never that easy.

The final third of the movie does kick into gear with the kidnapping of Lee Chan. When father Chan is contacted, the villains demand he turn over the remote control device if he wants to see his son alive again. Of course Chan risks his son's life by taking a phony device, which is actually a very crude tracking device that will lead the German police to the lair of the kidnappers. In a rapid-fire change of events, the device is at first accepted as being real, but the spies still plan to kill both Chans. When the device is finally revealed to be bogus, it buys the Chans a little more time, time enough for the police to surround the elaborate house. Again, the Olympic setting is nice, and the Berlin 1936 setting is always one of intrigue and mystery. However, Lee's role is minimal and even the inclusion of Layne Tom, Jr. as Charlie Chan, Jr. is almost too cute to be effective. For me this was run-of-the-mill Chan, but not one that particularly stands out.

As an added bonus, each Chan feature contains a wonderful documentary featuring film historians and clips, detailing one of the following four focus areas: Layne Tom, Jr. being interviewed about playing various sons of Charlie Chan in three of the movies; director H. Bruce Humberstone profiled by his quite young daughter; Keye Luke profiled by his grand-niece; and the entire Charlie Chan series profiled. The measure of success for any box set collection is the disappointment that even more Charlie Chan movies are not yet available at the end of this second collection. But more entries have already been released.

The Proud Ones
Movie: 2.5; Disc: 3.0
[Fox]

1956 wasn't a good year to be a Western unless you happened to be John Ford's *The Searchers*, one of the classic Westerns of all time. However, another Western released in 1956 was *The Proud Ones*, starring the always underrated Robert Ryan and Jeffrey Hunter, who also happened to co-star in *The Searchers*. Virginia Mayo comes along to provide romantic support to the Robert Ryan character. Supporting players include a bevy of recognizable names including Walter Brennan, Arthur O'Connell and smarmy Robert Middleton as the evil gambling villain, Honest John Barrett.

The movie is more a character study than an action fueled Western, but its CinemaScope and Deluxe Color (nicely restored) add a sense of depth and visual vastness to the proceedings. Robert Ryan is quite effective as the past middle-aged Marshal Cass Silver, a man who wishes to maintain the peace and live a non-eventful life. However, the West is expanding and the first cattle drivers are ready to invade the town to party. Flat Rock's business citizenry are just as anxious to greet the just-paid cattlemen, and they show their appreciation by doubling the prices of all their merchandise, anticipating fat times ahead.

However, two problems occur, besides the obvious one of drunken cattlemen with too much time and too much drink. First of all, corrupt gambler Honest John Barrett is opening a new gambling saloon in town, and Cass knows his methods of operation. Secondly, one of the drivers is Thad Anderson (Jeffrey Hunter), the son of a man Cass had to gun down in self-defense years ago, but Anderson believes the marshal gunned down his father in cold blood. Cass' current deputy quits at this crucial time, citing the fact his wife is about to go into labor. Cass, to assuage his own guilt, has to hire Thad as his deputy, to get the young wild kid back on track. Cass also wishes to prove to Thad that he was justified in gunning down his father

and that Cass wishes to be the boy's friend and mentor. In the meantime, Cass has been grazed in the head by a bullet, damaging his optic nerve, and he momentarily goes blind for short intervals, of course during the most inopportune time. As Cass is making his rounds at night, finding himself in the gun sites of hired killers, he has to evade his assassins with low vision, which only adds to the movie's suspense. Robert Ryan, best known for his portrayals of villains, here plays a troubled hero, with physical defects. And of course, by the movie's end, Thad becomes the new law in town as Cass retires.

The Proud Ones is not one of the best 1950s Westerns, but its political statements make it ambiguous and of interest. Robert Middleton plays the sleazy gentleman gambler Honest John Barrett. His reason for setting up shop in town at this time has everything to do with the increased patronage, due to the cattle drivers arrival. All the businessmen in town double their prices for their goods and see a new era of enterprise opening up before them. They turn their blind eyes away from the evil infiltrating their town and understand that Barrett's gambling establishment, rigged and corrupt, is not any worse than the price gouging they are guilty of. Cass, during the climax, confronts the business leaders and calls out each one of them for their greed and self-centeredness, and before Barrett and his hired guns are brought to justice, Cass makes it clear that he no longer wants to be the law for this corrupt community, with or without Barrett.

Darn if these 1950s Westerns don't always generate a larger message apropos for current times, and The Proud Ones gets by on its wonderful performances and ethical-layered plot that speaks the truth better than it realizes.

House of Strangers
Movie: 3.0; Disc: 3.5
[Fox]

House of Strangers, labeled #17 in the Fox Film Noir series, becomes a multi-layered story of family greed and disintegration, of changing times and older people's inability to adjust to such change. It is a noir that deals most fully with the American melting pot and how it both creates and destroys people. In a simple manner, the movie reminds me slightly of Francis Ford Coppola's Godfather saga, just in the sense of Old World tradition attempting to be hot-wired to the American experience, and the importance of family in establishing a successful business. But along with such financial success comes corruption, which attempts to destroy the family.

The cast of House of Strangers is uniformly strong. Edward G. Robinson plays Gino Monetti, the patriarch and president of his own bank, a jovial person that does not worry about collateral or intricate paper work. If Monetti trusts his neighborhood patron, that patron gets the loan no matter how risky the potential of repayment becomes. If Monetti does not personally approve of the loan, that patron does not get a dime. Monetti's four sons, three of them worthless hangers-on and conniving opportunists (Luther Adler, Efrem Zimbalist, Jr. and Paul Valentine), wait for the old man to die so they can inherit the family business and run it in the modern way, making even more money. The fourth son, Richard Conte as Max, is a lawyer and not involved in the family banking business, and he loves and is loved by his father. Following Old World tradition, Max is to be married to an attractive Italian-American girl (Debra Paget), but he falls for the hardened American woman Irene (Susan Hayward), who both manipulates him but also helps him to break free of familial chains and traditions. During one family dinner, citing business, Max sneaks out for a date with Irene, but not before Gino makes a wonderful speech comparing Old World ways to the American ways, and what it means to become an American.

As banking laws change, Gino gets investigated by the state and, because of his negligent record keeping, is indicted. However, innocent son Max takes the fall for

the family and serves seven years in prison, hating his brothers for their double-cross. Father Gino dies while Max is serving prison time, and once released, Max vows revenge, while Irene, who loves him, begs him to get on a plane for the opposite coast where he can start all over, free of the family skeletons and ghosts. In the exciting climax, the three brothers beat Max to a pulp and attempt to throw his semi-conscious body off a high-rise balcony. Tension only increases as the movie moves swiftly towards its conclusion. *House of Strangers* is a wonderful drama with noirish overtones (it seems as more and more of the Fox Noirs are released, more and more are borderline noir, which is still okay with me). The film is heavy on relationships, especially the ones comparing the freeloading dependent brothers to the one independent one, who has found success. Susan Hayward, playing the headstrong American woman who works to free Max of his father's obligation, such as the expectation to marry an Italian woman, is manipulative, sexy and controlling…but she always thinks of what's best for Max and her first, so her harshness is softened as she pleads for Max to forget revenge and simply start a new page in the book of his life. The three evil brothers, one of whom is conniving, cool as steel and innately evil, is contrasted to the generally stupid professional prizefighting brother and the quiet, easily influenced brother, who rides his greed on the coattails of the evil brother. And then there's Gino, the self-made Italian American, who is proud of what he has created in the New World, and proud that he can pass it on to his sons, who of course do not appreciate the gesture.

House of Strangers is not the best noir in Fox's series, but it is an involving drama of relationships, clashing customs and what a father's success does to children who never had to work their way out of the ghetto. The performances are the focus here.

Extras include audio commentary, a poster, still and photography gallery and trailers. Simply stated, no one does noir, not even Warner Bros., like 20th Century Fox.

Ring of Fear
Movie: 3.0; Disc: 3.5
[Paramount]

Ring of Fear is a hoot! It's not a great film by any sense, but it is a great entertaining popcorn movie from start to finish.

The 1954 film seems to be a B+ retread of *The Greatest Show on Earth*, released only two years earlier. And in 1954 *Ring of Fear* is one of the first movies released in the widescreen CinemaScope format, along with DeLuxe color. The cast includes Clyde Beatty and his traveling circus, and many times the film grinds to a halt to allow the master Beatty to show some of his lion-taming skills, apparently appealing to youngsters and the young at heart. Recently deceased author (creator of the Mike Hammer mystery-thriller series) Mickey Spillane appears as himself, constantly referring to his latest Mike Hammer novel and all the fame and fortune that has come his way. In a sense he is there to be the private eye and detective mastermind who can easily solve the case, but his part hasn't been developed beyond his what-the-hell-am-I-doing-here malaise. Circus owner Pat O'Brien has very little to do as well, other than chomp on his cigar and register one-note anger that his circus has been jinxed. Sean McClory as Dublin O'Malley, the homicidal maniac, at least gets to chew up the scenery, and he does so in fine Irish overkill mode that adds dramatic interest. In the film's opening minutes, Dublin breaks out of prison by punching his way out and jumping into a truck. Followed by authorities, Dublin makes it to the tracks where he hops a train to safety. However, being an intelligent homicidal maniac, he kills an innocent man and throws his body on the train tracks, in front of an oncoming train, to make it appear he has been killed. Now free, he does back to his old haunts, the Clyde Beatty circus, where nobody knows the slick showman has been doing time. At the circus he has his eye on his former flame, a high wire artist, but he has to scheme to get her husband out of the way, and he has to connive to get back his former job as Ring Master. He blackmails alcoholic circus worker Twichy (Emmett Lynn) into doing some of his dirty work, causing minor disasters to occur (fires break out unexpectedly, new circus rope breaks, etc.). When the guilt-ridden Twichy threatens to reveal the truth to authorities, Dublin drowns the pathetic weasel in a troth of water, making it appear the aging circus worker was drunk and fell in accidentally.

By the movie's end Mickey Spillane, wise to Dublin's antics, allows himself to be lured to Dublin's trailer, where he is almost killed, but of course this is not to be, even though the author of sleuth novels is almost blinded and tied up like a hog unable to squirm loose. Once Spillane is rescued and Dublin is revealed, Dublin frees a large circus cat to create a diversion, but this only allows Clyde Beatty one more moment of glory, and when Dublin hides in a train's boxcar and the savage beast soon follows, we know what the fate of Dublin will be.

Ring of Fear has something for everyone…the garish color of the circus with the widescreen chills and thrills, the excitement of seeing actual circus acts from the Beatty circus filmed (with classic cornball reaction shots of the same audience reacting to what they see), the suspenseful evil committed by an over-the-top Sean McClory as the murderous fiend and the thrill of seeing real-life celebrities such as Mickey Spillane and Clyde Beatty assume roles in the movie. As stated earlier, this is no *Greatest Show on Earth*, but *Ring of Fear* does provide harmless thrills for a matinee outing. For a thriller, the movie is almost warm and fuzzy when viewed today, and it still manages to entertain.

Lifeboat
Movie: 3.0; Disc: 3.5
[Fox]

By 1943 American audiences noticed director Alfred Hitchcock, and the director enjoyed a creative movie-making challenge.

Look at the premise of *Lifeboat*…six men and three women are the only survivors when a German U-boat sinks their ship, and one of the survivors is the Nazi captain that commanded the sneak attack. How can Hitchcock sustain interest for 90 minutes, without allowing the film to become too claustrophobic? Hitchcock filmed the entire movie in a tank of water using rear screen projection to create the seaside setting. Thus, the script by Jo Swerling (based upon John Steinbeck's story) must be character based and include enough tension to maintain the Hitchcock style. For the most part, the film succeeds admirably.

Star Tallulah Bankhead plays a photo journalist, but one who is most attracted to the societal/glamour side of the profession, a woman who always wears the stylish clothes and makeup, even while fighting for her life in the middle of the ocean. The plot focuses on her as the main character, for she is the only person in the lifeboat when the movie begins. As other survivors swim to the boat or are picked up floating in the water, we see Connie's (Bankhead's) reaction. Her running gag is that all her materialistic paraphernalia is singularly lost at sea…her camera, her luggage, her typewriter, and, just when the audience thinks she will crack as she loses all her "things," we instead are rewarded by her ability to adjust to such losses and still remain strong and courageous.

William Bendix, in one of his first roles, steals the show as the wounded Gus, the G.I. who has suffered a nasty cut to his leg, a wound that will soon turn gangrene and require amputation…at sea no less! Gus is young and carefree and speaks about the potential love of his life, Rosie, a young girl who lives to dance back home. Gus fears without both legs he will lose her to other eligible bachelors. Gus never complains, not even when the crew gives him a bottle of liquor to use to sedate him before surgery, and the surgeon will be the Nazi officer who hides a compass and a hidden bottle of water, while the others guess at the proper direction to row and suffer from thirst. In one of the more poignant scenes from the movie, Gus sees Willy's (Walter Slezak's) hidden water bottle, and before he can alert the others, the villainous Willy pushes Gus overboard and watches as the one-legged, weakened man struggles for his life, gradually disappearing beneath the choppy currents as good buddy Sparks (Hume Cronyn) awakens. It is at this point that the morally ambivalence we feel toward Willy (he is a dyed in the wool Nazi or is he a decent man trapped beneath a corrupt political system) becomes crystal clear…Willy is evil and self-serving.

However, later in the movie, after a final act of deception, the humane crew rises up and beats the Nazi to death and throws his body overboard, making the audience question ethical codes of right and wrong on both sides.

When the movie presents these intense characterizations being forced to make difficult decisions, the movie shines, but the film's conclusion, when a rear-projected enemy vessel threatens to cut the lifeboat in two, the limitations of such special effects become apparent and weaken the dramatic intensity somewhat.

Bottom line, *Lifeboat* is suspenseful and tension-filled from beginning to end, and the unique, well-drawn characters make the viewing audience care for them. The plot twists and turns make us question the rightness and wrongness of the specific decisions that people make, such as who is the leader and whether or not they are worthy. Even the director appears for one of his celebrated cameo appearances by turning up as the before-and-after subject of a weight-loss ad in a newspaper that one of the survivors is reading on the boat. Extras include audio commentary and a wonderful making-of documentary, as well as a still gallery and trailers.

All Through the Night
Movie: 3.0; Disc: 3.5
[Warner Bros.]

In 1942 Warner Bros. attempted to fuse its tough-guy gangster genre with its world-weary WW II spy genre. But if that wasn't enough, under the able guidance of director Vincent Sherman, *All Through the Night* also fused its hard-hitting dramatic tone with that of light-hearted comedy, to produce a true anomaly. Imagine Humphrey Bogart playing his typical dashing gangster role, here re-imagined as man-about-town (Broadway and 42nd Street based) gambler and sports promoter, Gloves Donahue. Donahue is worldly, tough, a ladies' man, but he's always surrounded by his entourage of light-hearted gangsters, played by wonderful character actors such as William Demarest, Jackie Gleason, Phil Silvers, Wally Ford and Frank McHugh. These hard-as-nails New Yorkers represent the lower-class rising (by hook or crook) to achieve success and live out the American dream. When Donahue's old-world German baker Miller, who produces the only cheesecake that Donahue will eat, is brutally murdered, the avenging angel Donahue discovers Miller was murdered because he was being strong-armed to help an underground group of Nazi spies attempt to blow up a U.S. naval vessel in the best fear-invoking terrorist manner. Donahue and company operate as an adult version of The Bowery Boys, with Bogart's deadly serious portrayal and occasional murder balancing out the comedic shenanigans and reminding the viewer that this is a deadly serious spy drama. On the Nazi side, we have Conrad Veidt as Ebbing, the suave German operations leader who is assisted by his muscle, Peter Lorre (Pepi), the equally suave piano player hit man. Martin Kosleck plays

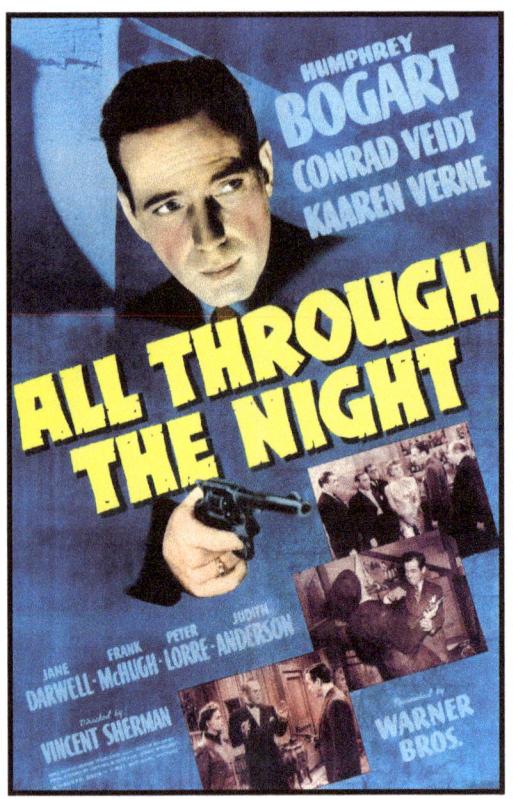

a Nazi sympathizer, and Judith Anderson is also one of the Fifth Columnists. Wow, what a terrific cast.

The movie features several stand-out sequences, including Bogart and Demarest investigating a spooky urban warehouse, with Demarest apprehended by the bad guys as Bogart investigates, Bogart not knowing his pal has been captured. This sequence leads to an intense battle aboard an open freight elevator with a fight to the death between Donahue and the Nazi muscle. Other sequences occur in the Nazi stranglehold, directly adjacent to the warehouse, where short wave radios are erected alongside portraits of Hitler and secret files. Even the grisly murder of Miller in his own shop cellar is creepy, with the evil Peter Lorre throwing the baker down the stairs and eventually hiding the corpse in a wooden bin, with only part of one hand hanging out.

What is most interesting about *All Through the Night*, besides the stellar cast, is the subtly switching tone that meanders from broad comic slapstick to blood-curdling suspense. (The sequence where Donahue enters the back exit of the nightclub, only to find tough guy club owner Barton MacLane stagger out of a back room and collapse from a gunshot wound, desperately trying to communicate to Donahue before he expires, is gripping cinema.)

Perhaps the sequence that best sums up these clashing tones is the sequence where Bogart and Demarest crash the secret Nazi meeting by knocking out and stealing the identification papers of two American Nazi sympathizers. Stern Nazi Martin Kosleck asks Bogart to give a full report on new progress. Realizing that Donahue is like a fish out of water, Demarest's Sunshine stands up, offers vocal support by employing some rapid-fire Nazi speak (which Donahue mimics and repeats), punctuated by his thrusting out of his arm in a Nazi salute, followed by Donahue doing the same, followed by the entire audience rising and thrusting in unison, demonstrating what devoted trained dogs these people have become. The sequence illustrates the expert comic timing created by Demarest, but it also shows the untapped comedic talent that Bogart brought to the table.

While *All Through the Night* is not a classic Warner Bros. drama, it is most definitely a riveting diversion and an absolutely delightful roller coaster suspense ride that features many memorable performances and gripping sequences. The movie only falls flat with the mediocre performance of leading lady Kaaren Verne, whose ambivalent Nazi supporter/nightclub singer never catches fire. But other than this one flaw, the movie is a visual delight.

Across the Pacific
Movie: 2.5; Disc: 3.5
[Warner Bros.]

Volume two of *The Humphrey Bogart Collection*, released by Warner Bros., includes many left-of-center Bogart entries, none of which measure up to *The Maltese Falcon* or even *All Through the Night*, but movies that are nonetheless entertaining. One year after directing *The Maltese Falcon*, director John Houston made *Across the Pacific*, again starring Humphrey Bogart with his *Maltese Falcon* co-stars Sydney Greenstreet and Mary Astor. This spy drama, literally culminating on December 7, 1941 in the Panama Canal Zone, is also a breezy romantic romp (less breeze and more spy tension would have improved the slowly-paced drama). The movie begins as Bogart's character Rick Leland is dishonorably discharged from the U.S. Army. Making clear his mercenary goals, Rick attempts to join the Canadian Army but is rejected, so he signs on as a hand on a slow boat to Asian.

In this relatively small cast, Leland meets Mary Astor's character of Miss Marlow, a woman that claims to be a merchandise buyer, who travels to Europe frequently. While Astor is pretty in a perky, cute sense, she is only a few years away from playing matrons and mothers and looks pretty long in the tooth for a woman described by Bogart as the type of woman men dream of possessing when they are 19 years old. And to play up her sexuality, Marlow appears throughout the movie in various stages of undress, to be more alluring to Leland (he gets her to partially open her cabin door, soap in her hair, obviously naked; Marlow appears sunbathing onboard the deck; Marlow delivers lines wearing her night clothes), but her sexuality is more mechanically created by lines in the script than by her inherent sensuality. Astor, whose character is worlds away from her femme fatale presence in *The Maltese Falcon*, plays comedy best in *Across the Pacific*. She is onstantly being pushed to the ground, quickly rising back up, her lipstick smeared. Clever lines of dialogue always seem to punctuate such slapstick diversions. In one sequence Marlow picks herself up and tells Rick she will retreat immediately to her cabin…so she can faint!

And the other familiar passenger is Sydney Greenstreet, playing Dr. Lorenz, a professor whose expertise is the culture of the Orient and, in particular, the Japanese, a people that he claims to love and respect a little too much—in the weeks prior to the Japanese invasion of Pearl Harbor. His political allegiance is never hidden, and from the get-go, the audience suspects Lorenz's evil intentions. As we slowly learn, Leland has not been discharged from the army but is working with U.S. intelligence agents to get into the good graces of Lorenz, so he can discover the robust man's anti-American

plans before they can be carried out. Affable Victor Sen Young (billed as Sen Young) plays goggle-eyed Japanese passenger Joe, a man who tries too hard to get into Leland's good graces. Of course later when Leland is about to get the drop on Lorenz, guess who pops out from behind the shadows to clunk Leland over the head? Lorenz ups the ante by using his cane twice to bash in Leland's face and head for good measure.

Once the movie moves to Panama and the espionage elements come to the forefront, especially when Leland's friendly agent Smith (Charles Halton) is brutally eliminated, the movie kicks into high gear. We learn that Lorenz has secretly shipped in airplane and bomb parts so the Panama Canal can be eliminated a day before the attack on Pearl Harbor occurs. Lorenz pledges complete allegiance to the Japanese powers. Once his plans have been foiled and he attempts to commit hari-kari in a visual metaphor of weakness, the man does not have the courage to take his own life and pleads for Leland to shoot him in the temple.

While the cast of Bogart, Astor, Greenstreet and Sen Young are outstanding and their interactions clever fun, the movie takes too long morphing from light romance to suspenseful spy drama. The film's exciting final third only attests to how lethargic the first two-thirds of the movie are. After *The Maltese Falcon*'s critical and popular success, John Houston's *Across the Pacific* seems disappointing and unfocused.

Thunder Road
Movie: 3.0; Disc: 3.5
[MGM]

Many people believe that Robert Mitchum never surpassed his performance as Max Cady in the underrated 1962 version of *Cape Fear*, one of the best suspense thrillers ever produced. Mitchum became Cady, demonstrating why the generally superb Robert DeNiro could not approximate Mitchum's inspired, natural performance from the original. Simply stated, DeNiro displays the artifice of his craft while Robert Mitchum breathes Max Cady. Spookily, it's as though Mitchum felt a bonding and closeness to the Cady character and truly understood the demons that the ex-con experienced. Cady is true evil but he's not externally the boogie man that DeNiro becomes. Mitchum reveals the dark underbelly of his soul in his cleverly non-chalant line delivery. Mitchum's entire body, the way he stands, the way he wears his hat, his sleepy eyes, the quiver of his mouth and his distinct body language all create one of the most consummate portrayals of evil the screen has ever seen.

Four years earlier, in a entirely different performance, Robet Mitchum appears to be piecing together the Max Cady persona in his co-written and starring role as Luke Doolin, in the exploitative *Thunder Road*. In this movie Robert Mitchum stars as a returning Korean War veteran, who takes over his family's moonshining business, as the principle delivery driver. Unfortunately the federal revenue people are hot on the interstate moonshiners' tail and want to close down the network. The feds do not actually want to bust the little hillbilly farmers; they want the syndicate gangsters who are muscling in. Jacques Aubuchon, as Carl Kogan, makes a deal for all the moonshiners to turn their operations over to him, and he will guarantee them a specific price per month. Mitchum spearheads the movement not to trust the city muscle and, though not unanimous, the farmers vote to reject the offer. Mitchum realizes that this means war and now the feds will be coming from one direction and the gangsters, with guns blazing, will be coming from the other.

Mitchum's Luke Doolin again has that white trash sneer and rebel attitude. Although he becomes the movie's hero, he is at worst an outlaw, a criminal, who is making money (as his family has done for generations, in an era before the revenue men even cared) from selling illegal substances. Might as well be drugs. In *Thunder Road* it's moonshine, just as illegal and just as criminal. Doolin likes to maintain his hangdog face with a droopy cigarette dangling from his threatening lips. So much of Max Cady exists in Luke Doolin, even if Doolin is basically a good guy. He is still a little man with a great deal of pride, being squished by the system, and he fights back with all the courage that exists inside.

James Mitchum, the eldest son of Robert, plays brother Robin in *Thunder Road*. James looks very much like his father, but beneath the hard exterior the younger Mitchum has an innocence and sweetness lurking under the surface. Luke Doolin swears that his brother Robin will never become a driver in the family business and that he will kill any person who involves him. Sultry Keely Smith (wife and singing partner of Louis Prima) provides the love interest, whose lethargy is conveyed by her torch-singing demeanor, performing sultry

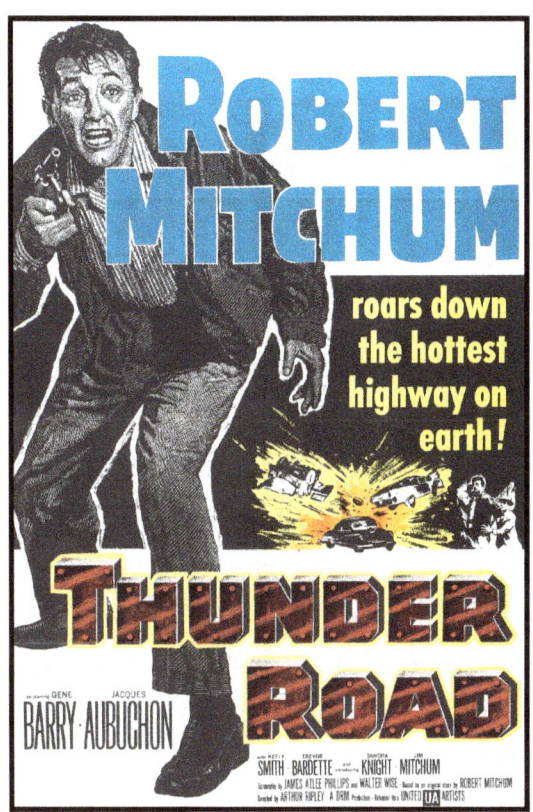

songs in rowdy bars and dives for very little money. One of the kindnesses shown her by Luke is their final meeting together, where Luke gives her $9,000 cash and a thinly disguised goodbye. Max Cady was similarly attracted to this type of nightclub women.

But Robert Mitchum's performance comes to life out on the rural roads as he is both pursued by the government boys and by the assassin outlaws. Keeping both hands on the wheel and a cool calmness, Luke Doolin examines his options carefully, as cold-blooded criminals are trying to drive him off the road. In a superb sequence, one of the gangsters passes Doolin as Doolin returns the favor and passes the assassin. When the two cars are side by side, each proud driver staring the other down, Doolin gets the final laugh by flicking a lighted cigarette into the gangster's face, causing the surprised driver to crash off the side of the road, his car flipping and catching fire. In another equally gripping sequence, Doolin twists around a curve to see two cars blocking the road. Instead of slowing to a stop, Doolin accelerates the engine, hitting the cars square in the middle, pushing them aside, as he continues full throttle ahead (with enough extensive body damage to put him out of action for three days).

In this era of the emerging anti-hero and the exploitation teenage film fare on the drive-in film circuit, *Thunder Road* delivers the goods (too bad the Robert Mitchum-

sung rock'n'roll hit 45-rpm record arrived after the movie hit theaters. The title song is only played in a slow, folk delivered version over the title credits and instrumentally throughout). Robert Mitchum's portrayal of Luke Doolin becomes an experimental canvas for pulling together all the complex components that would become Max Cady four years later. Think of the sneering, skinny youthful Elvis Presley without the innocence and cuteness. That's the point where Max Cady was born.

Mr. Moto Collection: Volume 2
Movies: *Mr. Moto's Gamble* (2.5);
Mr. Moto in Danger Island (3.0);
Mr. Moto Takes a Vacation (3.0);
Mr. Moto's Last Warning (2.5);
Disc: 3.5
[Warner]

The first Mr. Moto Warner Bros. box set was a revelation, standing directly alongside and holding its own against the equally impressive Warner Bros. Charlie Chan sets. In fact, I would rate the first Moto set as superior to the creaky, early Warner Oland Chans. However, it must be remembered that the Chans are being presented in chronological order, while the eight Moto movies are being presented out of sequence, with the first box set containing the stronger entries. The impressive amount that Warner Bros. spent (around two million dollars) restoring both the Motos and Chans only makes this rediscovery process (and for me watching the Moto films for the first time) all the richer.

Mr. Moto in Danger Island is a very strong second tier Moto and contains the most Gothic mood and spookiness of any of the four films in this second volume. By second tier I mean that Moto is no longer the dark and mysterious killer who will stab his enemy to death. Peter Lorre's portrayal of Moto is always mysterious, low-key and exuberant in manner and politeness, yet the Moto of the first few entries was more a secret agent trained to be ruthless and kill if necessary, and Moto shot, stabbed and tossed victims to their fitting demise. However, with the second tier Motos the formula of the B series kicked into gear. Moto remains mysterious but far less dangerous and ruthless. He was often given a comedic sidekick, in this case Warren Hymer as "Twister" McGurk, a professional wrestler with more heart than brains. When Moto offers some mentoring to his friend, demonstrating some judo flips, Twister, who defeats a wrestler portrayed by Ward Bond, is indebted to Moto and decides to accompany Moto to Puerto Rico, when Moto appears to become seriously ill. It seems Moto's predecessor was murdered and Moto must pick up the pieces of the case involving diamond smuggling. Moto, who is faking appendicitis, is expecting to be apprehended by the smugglers, and, with police help, he can capture them from the get-go. However, police arrive too late and the gang members escape after a rough and tumble free-for-all.

Of course the potential guilty parties include a close-knit group of the American-appointed governor (John Harvey); the elderly Colonel Castle (Charles D. Brown), who is in charge of the police department; his lovely daughter Joan (Amanda Duff); the governor's nephew George (Robert Lowery); Commissioner Madero (Leon Ames) and the mysterious Sutter (Jean Hersholt). All these people have motive and opportunity to commit murder and at various times each person (except love interest Joan) are photographed skulking around, peering in at the corners of rooms and in general playing the red-herring portrayal to perfection. Clever, unexpected murders abound, including the servant, who is electrocuted running the water for Moto's bath (an electrical booby-trap is wired to the tub). Soon the benevolent appearing Colonel Castle is found clutching a knife in the body of the dead governor, as the authorities arrive on the scene. An incriminating phone call Castle had with the Governor seals his fate. Investigating the small island where the earlier detective was killed, Moto and Twister come upon a camp where Castle and his daughter are hiding, Moto pretends to be a criminal that is merely impersonating Moto to get information from the criminals. Finally, aboard a small craft, Moto and his men pursue a smuggler's boat, one that is manned by the smuggler chief. After warnings from Moto not to kill the captain, Sutter fires and mortally wounds the man, who, if he recovers, will reveal the mystery and identify the big boss. Of course, this smuggler's fate becomes a major surprise and ploy for Moto to reveal the identity of the murderer, which is done in dramatic style in the closing, frantic minutes. The bonus featurette is a tracing of Moto's literary roots and a comparison of his personality as portrayed in the feature films contrasted to the books.

The second film in the collection is actually the third Moto film, sort of. *Mr. Moto's Gamble* started out as the latest entry in the Charlie Chan series, but a despondent Warner Oland, undergoing a messy divorce and suffering from depression, walked off the set, refusing to return to Set 6. After much effort the production was postponed and all the cast and crew sent home. Within a matter of weeks, the script was slightly tweaked, replacing Charlie Chan with Peter Lorre's Moto, and having Keye Luke as Lee Chan attend a college class on criminology, taught by Mr. Moto, who is a friend of Charlie Chan's. Unfortunately, using basically the same script and the same dialogue for Moto (which was written for Chan), the film suffers. While Oland's style lends itself to delivering those pearls of wisdom, these same aphorisms lack snap, crackle and pop when delivered by Moto. Chan, whose character is more lethargic and low-key, does not translate into the more kinetic and crafty Moto, who at times seems to lack the focus he commanded in the other Moto films. Chan still commands viewer attention underplaying the role; Moto seems lost. However, it is quite interesting to see Key Luke's enthusiastic Lee Chan work side by side with Moto, even though, once again, Moto is saddled with a comedic sidekick (perhaps one too many?) Maxie Rosenbloom, a former professional boxer that went into the entertainment business. Rosenbloom plays Knock-out Wellington, a slaphappy fighter, who is a kleptomaniac and never remembers where he stole what he steals (and he takes Moto's detective class to learn how to remember, so he can return stolen goods).

The mystery and the setting of the film, the boxing ring, makes a stellar set piece for all the action and mysterious festivities, as the world of big ring gambling leads to the mysterious death of a prizefighter that is poisoned during the fight. He cannot answer the bell for the next round. And the unknown criminal mastermind can make a quick bundle of money from the bets placed. The major sequences involve the fight itself, with the favorite boxer having a nasty cut over the eye opened, and after the weasel in his corner applies a compound to close the wound, the boxer drops dead during the next round. Later, during the film's climax, a pistol is

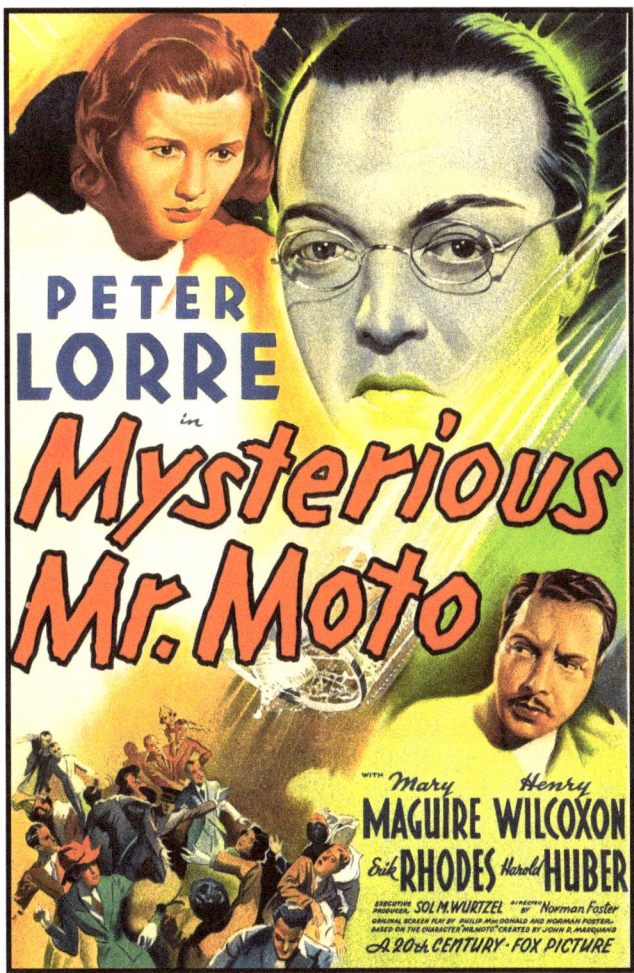

rigged beneath the ring with a timer, to fire at and kill a specific party at a designated time. While *Mr. Moto's Gamble* is thrilling and suspenseful, the pacing is a tad lethargic and a few more high-octane sequences would have helped. The featurette is perhaps the best of the collection, with the blow-by-blow description of how *Charlie Chan at the Ringside* became *Mr. Moto's Gamble*. It's truly fascinating cinematic history.

Mr. Moto's Last Warning, the next entry in the box set, returns to familiar Moto territory, with a screenplay co-written by Philip MacDonald and director Norman Foster, and Moto is played as far less the comic figure here. Moto's sense of danger is back.

In the political tensions of pre-war Europe, the British and French navies are venturing forth in joint maneuvers, but the threat of espionage threatens to strain relations between the two nations. Enter a shipboard phony Mr. Moto, who is working undercover with the actual Mr. Moto. The spy ring, seemingly headed by Eric Norvel (George Sanders), communicates its identity by flashing signals that contain specific symbols. Soon Norvel and his men offer the phony Moto a lift and take him to a specific alley-side house where he is killed. Norvel hooks up with ventriloquist Fabian the Great (Ricardo Cortez) and Danforth, a lanky bearded man (played by John Carradine), who is in reality an undercover British agent. Norvel and Fabian are the instigators of the naval sabotage plot, but the real Moto reveals himself to Danforth (actually named Richard Burke) and they agree to work together to bring the spies down. Moto, sporting plastic horned-rim glasses, poses as an Oriental art dealer.

In one of the most harrowing sequences of the entire Moto series, Burke's identity is discovered, and Danforth/Burke is invited aboard one of the spy-controlled salvage ships to view a formerly sunken ship, in a diving bell. Fabian even reveals their men are planting mines to blow up the French fleet. However, once underwater and 15-fathoms deep, Burke is told via radio that his identity is known, that he will be framed as the British agent targeting the French fleet and that his air supply has been cut off. In a slow, tortuous sequence, Burke slowly suffocates to death. Fabian suspects Moto's actual identity, and a secret bomb is hidden in his shop. While reading a telegram and fetching a book from a hidden panel in his floor, Moto hears a strange ticking, but his wall clock has stopped. Just in the tick of time Moto finds the package and throws the bomb through his window, where it explodes safely outside.

With the French fleet arriving the next day, Moto needs to act immediately and all the action converges in the spy warehouse where a free-for-all erupts with fists flying, people flipped in mid-air and Moto leaping through space. Moto is knocked unconscious and seemingly tied in a sack and lowered with rocks into the water, but his hands are already untied and he escapes easily. With the French fleet approaching in the distance, Fabian prepares to activate the underwater explosives and knocks Norvel unconscious, blowing up the mines before the ships arrive. In an action-filled confrontation, Moto and Fabian fight it out, until Fabian's girlfriend shoots him to death. With only a few laughs provided by author Rollo (Robert Coote), the film is deadly serious and becomes a first-rate spy programmer with plenty of action.

Heroic Mr. Moto confronts one of cinema's best villains/red herrings, Lionel Atwill.

The final entry is *Mr. Moto Takes a Vacation*, for me my favorite film in the second volume box set collection. Even though Peter Lorre and company were now making by-the-numbers formula entertainment, this last entry contains many of the elements that made the series so endearing.

Again Norman Foster directs from a script co-written by the director and Philip MacDonald, this time involving an unearthed Egyptian tomb and the discovery of the crown of the Queen of Sheba, a priceless artifact. Moto, again working undercover, accompanies the crown on a ship bound for the United States, to its new home at the Fremont Museum, curated by the perennial red-herring Lionel Atwill (Professor Hildebrand). The script features several bands of criminals vying to capture the crown, including a master criminal presumed dead and a gang of jewel thieves that are far less subtle and violently heavy-handed. Bumbling Brit Mr. Featherstone again supplies the comic relief, having the uncanny ability to let the cat out of the bag at the worst time (revealing Moto's actual identity aboard ship, thus alerting the criminal agents). Returning to the well one time too often (in a surprise plot twist already used in the series), once the crown arrives in America, it is loaded on an armored truck to be transported to the museum, but it turns out criminals waylaid the truck and the crown is immediately in criminal hands. But surprisingly, Featherstone and driver Willie Best recover the crown.

In a suspenseful sequence, as Moto wanders the Chinatown section of San Francisco purchasing popcorn from a street vendor, he is followed by a shadowy figure armed with a gun, who attempts to assassinate the International Policeman, who luckily is saved when someone steps in front of Moto. The criminal, agile and quick of foot, is able to scale the sides of buildings, jump from roof to roof and make his escape effortlessly. Moto concludes the criminal's agility proves that he is the presumed-dead master thief, now operating in America. Later that night, outside Moto's window in the rain, the stalker peeps into his hotel room to try to shoot the detective. However a phone call from Wong, a menial at the museum, pulls Moto to safety. When Moto utters his destination, the man-in-black rushes to the restaurant to silence Wong forever. Arriving at The Laughing Buddha, Moto finds Wong in a private curtained booth, dead, falling forward with a dazed expression, a knife in his back. Such sequences, photographed in nuanced shades of black, explain why this mystery/suspense series is so effective. Just as Moto is about to learn some important information, criminal elements intervene and keep the audience guessing, cinematography and editing becoming just as important as the acting.

Meanwhile, Hildebrand shows off his state-of-the-art security measures (invisible light beams, metal gates, electronic alarms) that will protect the Crown of Sheba against any sort of robbery attempt. But in clever plot twists, the system, at crucial times, is either defective, turned off or sabotaged by the criminal insider. In such sequences the all-so-worried Lionel Atwill is front and center and creates a fine supporting role. Compared to the delightfully klutzy Hildebrand, museum assistant Manderson (Joseph Schildkraut), elderly and limping using a cane, is always grumpy and pessimistic. Along with the gang of criminals that hang out at the camera shop in Chinatown, the movie contains a slew of red-herrings.

The film's climax, shot in darkness and shadows as is most of the movie, is bathed in rain that runs down every window and pelts every pavement, shot in darkness and shadows. Moto and Featherstone investigate the museum at night, tripping over mummy cases and ancient Egyptian treasures, as the camera pans boldly left, cutting across streaks of ambient light that only intensify the darkness and gloom. During this climax, the unidentified master criminal returns, stealing the crown, running through the museum and escaping momentarily by jumping through a huge plate-glass window to reach freedom outside. Moto figures out the identity of the criminal by cleverly looking at muddy footprints and drawing conclusions. To me *Mr. Moto Takes a Vacation* is the most Gothic and spooky mystery of the entire series, aided by creative set design and cinematography.

The final documentary covers the disappearance of Mr. Moto, as the series is halted due to anti-Japanese sentiments as the second World War approaches. However, as a B programmer series, Mr. Moto only becomes stronger over time, and these total eight features bring both a chuckle and thrill many years after their creation and release.

Editor's Final Note: So this concludes our first all color 40-page issue. Email me at midmargary@aol.com and let me know what you think, what you want to see more of, less of and how we could improve the magazine. We hope to see you again in six months... with your continued support!

www.ingramcontent.com/pod-product-compliance
Lightning Source LLC
Chambersburg PA
CBHW042030100526
44587CB00029B/4356